Watergate

Other titles in the American History series

AMERICAN HISTORY

Watergate

Michael V. Uschan

LUCENT BOOKS
A part of Gale, Cengage Learning

GALE
CENGAGE Learning™

Detroit • New York • San Francisco • New Haven, Conn • Waterville, Maine • London

LIBRARY OF CONGRESS CATALOGING-IN-PUBLICATION DATA

Uschan, Michael V., 1948-
  Watergate / by Michael V. Uschan.
    p. cm. -- (American history)
  Includes bibliographical references and index.
  ISBN 978-1-4205-0135-3 (hardcover)
  1. Watergate Affair, 1972–1974--Juvenile literature. 2. Nixon, Richard M. (Richard Milhous), 1913–1994--Juvenile literature. 3. United States--Politics and government--1969–1974--Juvenile literature. I. Title.
  E860.U835 2009
  973.924092--dc22
                                                                        2009005289

Lucent Books
27500 Drake Rd.
Farmington Hills, MI 48331

ISBN-13: 978-1-4205-0135-3
ISBN-10: 1-4205-0135-6

Printed in the United States of America
2 3 4 5 6 7 13 12 11 10

Printed by Bang Printing, Brainerd, MN, 2nd Ptg., 01/2011

Contents

Foreword

The United States has existed as a nation for over two hundred years. By comparison, Rome existed as a nation-state for more than a thousand years. Out of a few struggling British colonies, the United States developed relatively quickly into a world power whose policy decisions and culture have great influence on the world stage. What events and aspirations drove this young American nation to such great heights in such a short period of time? The answer lies in a close study of its varied and unique history. As American writer James Baldwin once remarked, "American history is longer, larger, more various, more beautiful, and more terrible than anything anyone has ever said about it."

The basic facts of U.S. history—names, dates, places, battles, treaties, speeches, and acts of Congress—fill countless textbooks. These facts, although essential to a thorough understanding of world events, are rarely compelling for students. More compelling are the stories in history, the experience of history.

Titles in the Lucent Books' American History series explore the history of the country and the experiences of its people. What influences led the colonists to risk everything and break from Britain? Who was the driving force behind the Constitution? What factors led thousands of people to leave their homelands and settle in the United States? Questions like these do not have simple answers; by discussing them, however, we can view the past as a more real, interesting, and accessible place.

Students will find excellent tools for research and investigation in every title. The American History series provides not only facts, but also the analysis and context necessary for insightful critical thinking about history and about current events. Fully cited quotations from historical figures, eyewitnesses, letters, speeches, and writings bring vibrancy and authority to the text. Annotated bibliographies allow students to evaluate and locate sources for further investigation. Sidebars highlight important and interesting figures, events, or related primary source excerpts. Time lines, maps, and full-color images add another dimension of accessibility to the stories being told.

It has been said that the past has a history of repeating itself, for good and ill. In these pages, students will learn a bit about both and, perhaps, better understand their own place in this world.

Important Dates at the

1960
Cuba establishes ties with the Soviet Union; Cuban dictator Fidel Castro seizes American assets on the island.

June 17, 1972
Five men are arrested at 2:30 A.M. for breaking into the offices of the Democratic National Committee at the Watergate complex.

November 22, 1963
President John F. Kennedy is assassinated in Dallas, Texas.

1960	1963	1966	1969	19

April 4, 1968
Civil rights leader Martin Luther King Jr. is assassinated in Memphis, Tennessee.

November 5, 1968
Richard M. Nixon is elected president of the United States.

September 5, 19
Palestinian terrori kidnap and murd eleven Israeli athle at the Olym Games in Muni Germa

1969
American astronauts Neil Armstrong and Edwin Aldrin become the first people to set foot on Earth's moon.

Time of Watergate

April 1973
The first handheld cellular phone call is made in New York City.

May 17, 1973
The Senate Watergate committee begins its nationally televised hearings; one day later attorney general–designate Elliot Richardson names Archibald Cox as the Justice Department's special prosecutor to investigate the Watergate burglary.

1974
India detonates its first nuclear weapon.

July 27, 1974
The House Judiciary Committee votes to impeach President Nixon.

April 22, 1994
Former president Richard M. Nixon dies.

1980
The United States boycotts the summer Olympics in Moscow.

| 1975 | 1978 | 1981 | 1984 | 1994 |

October 6, 1973
Syria and Egypt launch a combined attack on Israel; the conflict comes to be known as the Yom Kippur War, also called the October War.

August 8, 1974
President Nixon becomes the first U.S. president to resign; Vice President Gerald R. Ford becomes president.

September 8, 1974
President Ford pardons Nixon for any crimes he may have committed as president.

1975
Pol Pot and the Khmer Rouge seize control of Cambodia.

November 17, 1973
President Nixon claims he is innocent in Watergate, declaring "I'm not a crook."

The Political Scandal That Ousted a President

Four days after he suffered a massive stroke, former U.S. president Richard M. Nixon died on April 22, 1994, at the age of eighty-one in New York City. The funeral service for the thirty-seventh president of the United States was held April 27 at the Nixon Presidential Library & Museum in Yorba Linda, California. Hundreds of friends and public officials gathered to honor Nixon. Among them were dignitaries representing eighty-five nations and all four surviving former U.S. presidents— Gerald Ford, Jimmy Carter, Ronald Reagan, and George H.W. Bush.

In remarks delivered while standing with his predecessors, President Bill Clinton praised Nixon for a long political career that, in addition to his tenure as president, included terms as a U.S. representative, senator, and vice president. Clinton acknowledged that Nixon had made many mistakes, but he expressed the hope that people would also

remember Nixon for his many accomplishments. Clinton said, "Today is a day for his family, his friends and his nation to remember President Nixon's life in totality. To them let us say, may the day of judging President Nixon on anything less than his entire life and career come to a close."[1]

Despite Clinton's gracious words, that day had not arrived. A national poll at the time of Nixon's death showed that only 27 percent of Americans predicted future historians would consider Nixon a great president while 44 percent believed he would be remembered as a dishonored leader. Nixon's dishonor reached its climax some twenty years earlier on August 9, 1974, the day he became the first, and so far, the only U.S. president to resign from the nation's highest office.

Nixon resigned because of the Watergate scandal. And even two decades later when he died, many Americans were still unable to forget or forgive Nixon's involvement in what is considered the worst presidential scandal in U.S. history.

A Burglary and Cover-up

Up until June 1972, not many people outside of Washington, D.C., had heard of Watergate, a complex of six buildings which house a fashionable hotel, offices, apartments, and a retail center with stores and restaurants. That changed after five men—Bernard L. Barker, Virgilio R. Gonzalez, Eugenio R. Martinez, Frank A. Sturgis, and James W. McCord Jr.—were arrested in the early hours of June 17 for breaking into the office of the Democratic National Committee.

The incident seemed to be only a minor burglary at first. But it soon became famous around the nation and the world as hundreds of stories in newspapers and on television began linking the break-in to President Richard Nixon's presidential campaign. Nixon, a Republican, was running for a second term against Democratic senator George McGovern of South Dakota.

News reports said that the men who were arrested were working for the Committee to Re-Elect the President (CRP), a fund-raising organization created by Nixon. Their mission had been to steal information on how the Democrats were planning to defeat Nixon. The bungled

Before the scandal, "Watergate" was just the name of a fancy hotel and office complex in Washington, D.C.

burglary became even more important when investigators learned that McCord was a security coordinator for CRP and that two accomplices who were arrested later—G. Gordon Liddy and E. Howard Hunt—had once been members of Nixon's White House staff.

Former U.S. attorney general John Mitchell headed CRP. Fearful that a full investigation of the incident would doom Nixon's chances to be reelected, Mitchell and Jeb Magruder, his top assistant, decided that the best way to handle the burglary was to conceal White House involvement in it. That decision was made the day after the burglary.

The cover-up eventually involved not only Mitchell and other top campaign officials, but also members of Nixon's White House staff and the president himself. This illegal effort included destroying evidence; lying to law enforcement officials, judges, and members of Congress; and attempts to force the Federal Bureau of Investigation (FBI) to quit looking into the incident. According to author Fred Emery in his book, *Watergate: The Corruption of American Politics and the Fall of Richard Nixon*, it was the cover-up, and not the break-in itself, that forced Nixon to resign. Emery writes, "It was a pattern of malfeasance [misconduct] by him [Nixon] and his men that led to [Nixon having to leave office]."[2]

Two Intrepid Reporters

The attempted cover-up went on for nearly two years. It failed partly because two *Washington Post* newspaper reporters refused to quit investigating the burglary. Carl Bernstein and Bob Woodward stuck with the story for many months to uncover how White House officials had illegally tried to conceal White House participation in Watergate. They also turned up evidence that the Nixon administration had, in the past, illegally monitored telephone conversations of private citizens and government officials for political purposes. They also discovered that the White House had authorized another burglary in 1971 to gain the medical records of a government worker who had leaked secret papers on the Vietnam War to a newspaper.

Bernstein and Woodward, however, were only catalysts who ignited more historic actions by government officials. Their newspaper stories and a growing public anger over the effort to cover up the political scandal that became known as Watergate led a Senate committee in May 1973 to formally investigate the burglary. In nationally televised hearings, the Senate Watergate committee questioned top White House staff members and gained access to transcripts and tape recordings of talks between the president and his staff concerning Watergate. The Senate investigation led to new revelations about what happened, including details on Nixon's involvement in the cover-up.

The committee unearthed so much damaging information about Nixon that the House Judiciary Committee began proceedings to impeach him for obstructing justice on July 27, 1974. Impeachment is the power the Constitution gives Congress to charge and try a president who breaks the law.

The relentless investigation of reporters Bob Woodward (right) and Carl Bernstein (left) into the Watergate scandal revealed the cover-up by the Nixon Administration.

Less than two weeks later, on August 8, 1974, Nixon resigned as president. He believed resigning would be less disgraceful than being tried, found guilty, and thrown out of office by Congress. The next day, Nixon left the nation's capital and Vice President Gerald R. Ford took over as president.

"A Little Thing"

The irony of Watergate is that many historians believe Nixon would not have had to surrender the presidency if he had been honest about his involvement in the burglary and not tried to conceal it. Historians believe Americans were angrier about Nixon's dishonesty than about the burglary itself. Historians also claim that most people would have accepted the burglary as simply another of the dirty political tricks both parties had often committed against each other if Nixon and his aides had not tried to cover it up.

In a 1977 television interview with British journalist David Frost, Nixon admitted that he never thought trying to cover up Watergate would get him into trouble. "[I] screwed up terribly in what was a little thing that became a big thing,"[3] said Nixon. However, the "little thing"—the burglary—led directly to the "big thing"— the cover-up that wound up making Nixon the first president to leave office in disgrace.

Chapter One

President Richard M. Nixon

George Reedy, press secretary for President Lyndon B. Johnson, said that the presidency is such a difficult job that it brings out the best or worst in the person who has the job. "The office neither elevates nor degrades a man," Reedy claimed. "What it does is to provide a stage upon which all his personality traits are magnified and accentuated."[4]

Such character traits are seen when a president handles tough issues. Nixon is credited with having courage in speeding up school integration in the South, where blacks were slowly beginning to attend school with whites following civil rights gains in the 1960s. Although Nixon had been a belligerent anti-Communist for decades, he was flexible enough as president to ease tensions with Communist countries by visiting the Soviet Union and People's Republic of China. Nixon also created the Environmental Protection Agency to deal with environmental concerns.

However, historians believe some elements of Nixon's personality led him to make bad decisions. Nixon campaigned for president in 1968 by promising voters that he would quickly end the Vietnam War, but his unwillingness to admit military defeat once he was in office allowed the conflict to continue for five more years. Many historians believe that several flaws in Nixon's character led to Watergate. These flaws included his inability to trust people, his desire to punish his critics, and his willingness to use unethical or illegal methods to win elections.

The character traits that made Nixon successful, such as his ability to work harder than almost anyone else and his fierce desire to always succeed, as well as those which doomed his presidency were forged while Nixon was growing up and during his early political campaigns.

A Harsh Childhood

Richard Milhous Nixon was born on January 9, 1913, in Yorba Linda, California. Richard's parents, Francis (Frank) A. Nixon and Hannah Milhous Nixon, were Quakers, and they opposed war and condemned drinking and smoking. In 1922 the family's 12-acre (9 ha) lemon grove failed, so the family moved to Whittier, California, where Frank started a combination grocery store and gas station.

Richard, his four brothers, and mother all worked in the family business. When Richard was in high school, he woke up every day at 4 A.M. and drove to nearby Los Angeles to buy fresh vegetables. He washed them and set them out for customers before going to school. Nixon learned valuable lessons from his father. "He left me a respect for learning and hard work; and the will to keep fighting no matter what,"[5] Nixon wrote as an adult.

The Nixons were poor despite their hard work. "We had very little," Nixon claimed. "I wore my brother's shoes, and my brother below me wore mine. We never ate out—never. We certainly had to learn the value of money."[6] Families struggling financially at this time was common because of the Great Depression, the economic downturn that began in 1929 and lasted more than a decade. Richard, however, felt humiliated because of his hand-me-down attire, and he resented people who looked down on him because of his poverty. He also had difficulty making friends because he was shy, which made him feel like an outsider. According to Nixon, his childhood experiences made him determined to

Richard Nixon, standing far right in this family portrait, with his parents and two brothers.

show people who snubbed him that he could be successful. In a 1974 interview, Nixon explains:

What starts the process, really, are laughs, slights and snubs when you are a kid. Sometimes it's because you're poor, or Irish or Jewish or Catholic or ugly or simply that you are skinny. But if you are reasonably intelligent and if your anger is deep enough and strong enough, you learn you can change those attitudes by excellence, personal gut performance, while those who have everything are sitting on their fat butts.[7]

Nixon channeled his inner anger into becoming a top student. He then attended Whittier College in his hometown with hopes of becoming rich and famous.

College Life

Nixon was able to attend Whittier College because his wealthy maternal grandfather had started a scholarship there for family

Stealing Cookies

One of the legends about George Washington, the first president of the United States, is how honest he was even as a young boy. A mythical story about Washington claims that when George's father asked him if he had cut down a cherry tree, the future president truthfully admitted he did it with a hatchet. George's father forgave him because he told the truth, and the story symbolizes that it is always best not to lie. A similar childhood incident involving Richard M. Nixon had a different outcome. John Sears, an aide to Nixon when he was president, describes Nixon's childhood experience in the book, *The Arrogance of Power* by Anthony Summers. According to Sears,

one day, Hannah Nixon baked some cookies. Little Richard saw those cookies and ate one of them. And she said, "Richard, did you eat that cookie?" He didn't know any better than to say yes, and she beat the daylights out of him, or maybe his father did when he came home. But Richard Nixon learned one thing from that: He would probably still have gotten the daylights beaten out of him if he'd said no. But when he'd admitted it [he was beaten and] totally rejected. That was a lifelong lesson to him.

Quoted in Anthony Summers, *The Arrogance of Power: The Secret World of Richard Nixon*. New York: Viking, 2000, p. 8.

Richard Nixon graduated from college in 1934 and won a scholarship to Duke Law School.

members. His scholarship made Nixon feel like a second-class student compared to students whose parents paid for their tuition. His feeling of being an outsider was heightened when the Franklins, a literary and social club at Whittier, rejected his membership application. Bitter about the rejection, Nixon then started a club he dubbed the Orthogonians; the name came from a Greek word meaning "upright." Nixon once said of the two groups, "They [Franklins] were the haves and we were the have-nots."[8]

Nixon was determined to prove to the Franklins he was as good as they were. He studied furiously and honed his speaking skills on the debate team. He also won election as president of the student body by promising to eliminate a ban on student dances. Ola Florence Welch, his college girlfriend, claims Nixon was unhappy, She said, "He seemed so lonely and so solemn at school. He didn't know how to mix. He was smart and sort of set apart. I think he was unsure of himself, deep down."[9] Nixon played football, his favorite sport, but was not very good and mostly rode the bench.

Nixon finished second in his 1934 graduating class and won a scholarship to Duke Law School in Durham, North Carolina. Nixon had to work in the school library for spending money, which again made him feel inferior to students who had money. Nixon dealt with this by spending so much time studying that fellow students nicknamed him "Iron-Butt." Nixon was so worried about his grades that he once broke into a dean's office to see what marks he was getting. Even though Nixon was not popular, he was elected president of his law school bar association in 1936 because students respected his intellectual achievements.

Meeting Pat

In 1937 Nixon graduated third in his class at Duke Law School. Nixon had dreamed of working for a big New York law firm, but he failed to get such a high-paying position. He was also rejected by the Federal Bureau of Investigation (FBI) when he applied for a job as an agent. Feeling defeated, the twenty-four-year-old Nixon returned to Whittier, California, to work for Wingert and Bewley, a small, local law firm.

A year later Nixon auditioned for and won a part as a college student in *The Dark Tower*, a play being produced by a local theater group. Some Nixon biographers claim that he did it to meet prospective clients and show his involvement in community affairs. During the play Nixon met Thelma Catherine Ryan, who would become his wife. Ryan was a schoolteacher known to friends as "Pat," because she was born on March 16, the day before St. Patrick's Day. They began dating and were married in a Quaker ceremony on June 21, 1940, in Riverside, California.

Naval Officer and Congressman

Nixon was not content being a small-town lawyer. In October 1941, he was offered a position in Washington, D.C. with the new Office of Price Administration, a federal agency created by President Franklin Roosevelt to regulate consumer goods prices and impose rationing programs. The agency was needed because the availability of products and their prices were being affected by World War II which was currently being waged in Europe. Nixon jumped at the chance to leave Whittier for new opportunities in Washington.

Two months later on December 7, Japan bombed Pearl Harbor in Hawaii and the United States entered World War II. Nixon decided to fight for his country, and in April 1942 he joined the U.S. Navy, even though his Quaker faith opposed military service. "It was a difficult decision for me to make," Nixon admitted, "but I felt that I could not sit back while my country was being attacked."[10] Nixon served as a ground operations officer, supervising movements of supplies and men from island to island as U.S. forces advanced through the Pacific to defeat Japan.

When Nixon was discharged from service in 1945, he decided to run for Congress in California as a Republican in the 1946 election. His opponent was Democrat Jerry Voorhis, who had held the seat since 1936. The election was dominated by the Cold War, the political, economic, and military conflict between Communist nations and democratic nations led by the United States that dominated the second half of the twentieth century.

Nixon took advantage of the American public's anti-Communist feelings at the time to defeat Voorhis. He claimed Voorhis was supported by pro-Communist groups, had favored the Soviet Union in votes in Congress, and believed in Communist ideals. Voorhis actually opposed communism, and historians say Nixon falsified claims against the Democrat to win. Years later even Nixon admitted his attacks had been unethical. He said, "Of course, I know Jerry Voorhis wasn't a Communist. I suppose there was scarcely ever a man with higher ideals than Jerry Voorhis, or better motivated. But I had to win. That's the thing you don't understand. The important thing is to win."[11]

"Tricky Dick"

Nixon continued his anti-Communist crusade in Congress as a member of the House Un-American Activities Committee (HUAC). The committee held hearings to identify Communist spies or sympathizers in the United States. On August 3, 1948, Whittaker Chambers, a former Communist Party member, claimed Alger Hiss was a Communist. Hiss was a former State Department official who had helped establish the United Nations.

Hiss testified before the committee two days later that he had never been a Communist or met Chambers. Nixon, however, believed Hiss had been evasive in his testimony and was lying. Nixon said, "I saw that he had never once said flatly, 'I don't know Whittaker Chambers.'"[12] At Nixon's request, the HUAC kept questioning Hiss until he finally admitted he had

Alger Hiss being sworn in to testify. Nixon became a hero in the fight against communism after getting Hiss to admit he lied on the stand.

known Chambers. Hiss was found guilty of perjury for lying to the committee and sentenced to five years in prison.

Nixon's exposure of Hiss made him a hero in the fight against communism, and in 1950 he used that notoriety to run for a vacant U.S. Senate seat. His opponent was Democrat Helen Gahagan Douglas, another California U.S. representative. Although Douglas opposed communism, she had once voted against funding for the HUAC because she did not feel communism was a threat to the United States. Nixon claimed that because of that vote, Douglas was a Communist sympathizer.

He also made other false claims about Douglas being a Communist, some of them quite clever. Because the color red was associated with communism, Nixon nicknamed Douglas the "pink lady" and claimed she was "pink right down to her underwear."[13] His campaign also sent out five hundred thousand fliers on pink paper unfairly accusing Douglas of associating with a New York congressman who had been linked to Communists. Nixon campaign signs even said: "If you want to Work for Uncle Sam [the U.S. government] Instead of Slave for Uncle Joe [Soviet leader Joseph Stalin], Vote for Richard Nixon."

Douglas was so upset at Nixon's campaign tactics that she labeled him "Tricky Dick" (Dick is a nickname for Richard), a nickname that he carried the rest of his life. But the shoddy tactics worked and Nixon was elected.

Vice President Nixon

Nixon once told a friend that he ran for the Senate because "the House offered too slow a road to leadership, and I went broke."[14] It did not take long for Nixon to make another big step politically. In the summer of 1952 presidential candidate Dwight D. Eisenhower, the U.S. Army general who helped win World War II, chose Nixon as his running mate because of his strong anti-Communist credentials.

After being nominated, however, Nixon was hit with allegations that he was illegally paying his personal expenses with campaign funds. Fearing that Eisenhower would drop him, Nixon made the bold move of defending himself in a televised speech on September 23, 1952. Since politicians can use campaign contributions for political purposes, such as travel expenses, Nixon told viewers that "every penny of it [campaign contributions] was used to pay for political expenses that I did not think should be charged to the taxpayers of the United States."[15]

Although his critics claimed Nixon did not answer the allegations that he used campaign funds for personal expenses, his speech was so effective that the public believed he had not done anything wrong. Eisenhower retained him as his running mate, and on November 4 they won the election.

For two terms from 1953 to 1960, Nixon was a strong, active vice president who enhanced the power and prestige of a position that had previously been unimportant. This was partly because Nixon was the first vice president required to temporarily run the government after Eisenhower became incapacitated by illness. Nixon briefly took over the duties of president when Eisenhower had a heart attack on September 24, 1955, a bout with ileitis (an intestinal infection) in June 1956, and a stroke on November 25, 1957. Nixon handled presidential duties, such as conducting meetings of the National Security Council, the experts who advise the president on foreign affairs.

Nixon was also highly visible to the entire world in a half-dozen trips he made to Europe, Latin America, and the Middle East to gain the support of foreign countries for U.S. policies. On July 24, 1959, he claimed democracy was superior to communism in a spirited debate with Soviet leader Nikita Khrushchev in Moscow, Russia. It was called the Kitchen Debate, because it took place in a kitchen that was part of an exhibit at the American Embassy about how U.S. citizens lived. Americans admired Nixon because he seemed heroic by debating with the Soviet leader. Nixon was also considered a hero on May 9, 1958, when he remained calm after anti-American protesters threw rocks at his limousine

The Checkers Speech

On September 23, 1952, Richard M. Nixon appeared on television to defend himself against charges that he had illegally used campaign funds to pay for personal expenses. He convinced voters he had not done anything wrong, partly because of the skillful way in which he talked about his love for his wife and children. Nixon's speech became known as the "Checkers speech" because of the masterful way he talked about a family pet as an example of his honesty. Here is an excerpt from Nixon's speech:

> We did get something, a gift.... A man down in Texas heard Pat on the radio mention the fact that our two youngsters would like to have a dog, and, believe it or not, the day before we left on this campaign trip we got a message from Union Station in Baltimore, saying they had a package for us. We went down to get it. You know what it was? It was a little cocker spaniel dog, in a crate that he [the man] had sent all the way from Texas, black and white, spotted, and our little girl Tricia, the six year old, named it Checkers. And you know, the kids, like all kids, loved the dog, and I just want to say this, right now, that regardless of what they say about it, we are going to keep it.

Richard M. Nixon, Checkers speech, September 23, 1952, History Place Great Speeches Collection, www.historyplace.com/speeches/nixon-checkers.htm.

and threatened his life when he visited Lima, Peru, and Caracas, Venezuela.

Eisenhower appreciated Nixon's work as vice president. He once wrote to Nixon: "You have brought to the office of Vice President a real stature that formerly it had not known."[16] Nixon gained so much experience that he believed he deserved to be the next president. So in 1960, he ran against John F. Kennedy, the Democratic nominee.

Nixon Loses Two Elections

Nixon was the favorite in the 1960 presidential election, because many people believed his service as vice president

Nixon's experience opposing communism caused Dwight Eisenhower, right, to pick him as his vice-presidential running mate in 1952.

The Power of Television

The very first televised debate between presidential candidates occurred on September 26, 1960. Television in 1960 was still a relatively new medium, but it was growing in the power it had to influence people about major issues, such as elections. In his book, *The Making of the President 1960*, historian Theodore H. White claims—as do many other historians—that the first debate between John F. Kennedy and Richard M. Nixon was key to Kennedy's victory. White writes that both candidates talked intelligently about their plans for the future but that Kennedy was more appealing to viewers because of the way he looked. White describes how the candidates looked on television:

> Kennedy was calm and nerveless in appearance. The vice president, by contrast, was tense, almost frightened, at turns glowering and, occasionally, haggard-looking to the point of sickness. [Nixon] has a broad, almost sunny smile when he is with friends. His is a broad open face and the deep eye wells, the heavy brows, the broad forehead give it a clean, masculine quality. Yet on television, the deep eye wells and the heavy brows cast shadows on the face and his eyes glowered on the screen darkly; when he became rhetorically indignant, the television showed ferocity; when he turned, his apparently thin brush of hair showed in a glimmering widow's peak.

Theodore H. White, *The Making of the President 1960.* New York: Atheneum, 1961, p. 186.

made him more qualified than Kennedy to be president. But Kennedy was attractive, charismatic, a hero of World War II, and an eloquent speaker, and those factors made him a formidable candidate.

On September 26, 1960, Nixon and Kennedy met for the first of four televised debates. Both candidates effectively defended their positions on issues, but Kennedy appeared handsome, strong, and confident while Nixon seemed nervous and looked tired because he had been sick for two weeks

with a knee infection. A national poll the next day showed 43 percent of viewers believed Kennedy had won the debate and 23 percent thought Nixon won.

The election was one of the closest in history and Kennedy won by only 114,673 votes out of more than 68 million cast. Nixon, in fact, could have won if 32,500 Kennedy votes had gone to him—4,500 in Illinois and 28,000 in Texas. Those votes would have given Nixon victories in those states and their 51 electoral votes he needed to win the presidency. Many

Nixon looked nervous and tired while John F. Kennedy, right, looked confident and handsome during their live television debate in 1960. Viewers responded more positively to Kennedy, which was a factor in Nixon's defeat in the election.

people thought Nixon should have challenged the balloting in those states because of widespread reports of improper voting. Nixon reportedly wanted to file a challenge but heeded advice from Eisenhower, who told him not to because it would create intense political division that could weaken the country. The loss left Nixon bitter. It also made him more willing to do anything to win an election. "I vowed," Nixon said, "that I would never again enter an election at a disadvantage by being vulnerable to them [his opponents]—or anyone—on the level of political tactics."[17]

Nixon returned to California where he practiced law and wrote *Six Crises*, a book about his long career in politics. The book became a bestseller, boosting his fame and leading Republicans to ask him to run for governor of California in 1962 against Governor Pat Brown. When

Nixon lost by three hundred thousand votes, most people believed his political career was over. Nixon seemed to confirm that the night of his defeat in an angry tirade against newspaper reporters, who he blamed for his defeat because of stories they wrote about his candidacy. He bitterly told reporters, "You won't have Nixon to kick around anymore, because, gentlemen, this is my last press conference."[18]

The "New Nixon"

Nixon moved to New York and became a partner in a prestigious law firm. Despite his vow to quit politics, Nixon campaigned heavily for Arizona senator Barry Goldwater in 1964 when he unsuccessfully ran against Democratic president Lyndon B. Johnson. Nixon's efforts raised his stature with fellow Republicans so much that in 1968 he decided to run again for president.

To improve his image as a bitter loser, Nixon tried to recast himself as the "New Nixon," someone who was more open and understanding of the problems of average Americans. Historian Theodore White writes, "the snarl and self-pity were gone and [what Nixon was showing now] was genuine and authentic; true to the inner man."[19] He tried to show his new common touch by appearing on the hit television comedy, *Laugh-In*, where he said "Sock it to me!" one of the show's humorous catchphrases that had become popular with viewers.

The Vietnam War, which had divided the nation, was the main issue in the election. Four years after winning election as president, Johnson was so unpopular for sending hundreds of thousands of Americans to fight there that on March 31, 1968, he announced he would not run for reelection. Vice President Hubert H. Humphrey won the Democratic nomination and Alabama governor George Wallace was the presidential candidate for the new American Independent Party, one of the strongest independent parties in U.S. history.

Nixon believed the United States should continue fighting and win the conflict. But to win supporters, Nixon said he knew how to bring the war to an end quickly. Claiming that it could hurt ongoing talks with North Vietnam to end the war, Nixon never revealed details of how he would achieve peace. This led some reporters to write that Nixon had a "secret plan" to end the war. Nixon, however, never had a specific strategy for achieving peace. In his memoirs he writes, "I never said that I had a 'plan,' much less a 'secret plan,' to end the war. I was deliberately straightforward about the difficulty of finding a solution. As I told the AP [Associated Press] on March 14, 1968, there was 'no magic formula, no gimmick [to end it].' "[20]

But many voters thought Nixon had such a plan and that belief helped him win the election.

"The Good and Bad Alike"

The president of the United States wields tremendous power, so much that a president's decisions affect people not only in the United States but also in nations around the world. Nixon himself loved wielding that power. In 1982 Nixon commented on how such power can be used by both good leaders and bad leaders. He said, "The good and bad alike can be equally driven, equally determined, equally skilled, equally persuasive. Leadership itself is morally neutral; it can be used for good or ill."[21]

Many historians believe Nixon misused his presidential power, and Watergate has become an enduring symbol of how he did that.

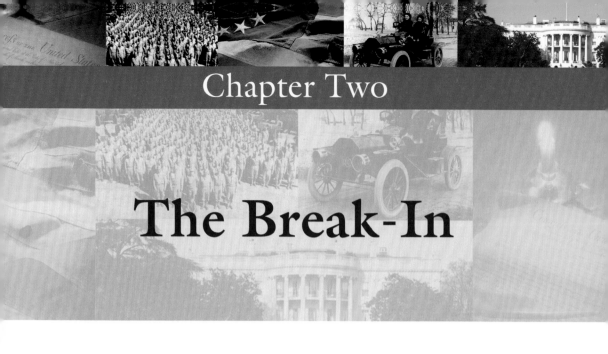

Chapter Two

The Break-In

On January 20, 1969, Richard M. Nixon was sworn in as the nation's thirty-seventh president. In his inaugural speech, Nixon commented only indirectly about the Vietnam War, a conflict that was dividing the nation more severely than at any time since the Civil War (1861–1865). Nixon never mentioned the war by name even though he had been elected partly because of his claim that he could quickly and honorably end it. But people who voted for Nixon because of that were heartened when he said, "the greatest honor history can bestow is the title of peacemaker." Nixon acknowledged, however, it would be difficult to end the bitter conflict. "We are caught in war, wanting peace," he said. "We are torn by division, wanting unity."[22]

Tens of thousands of people lining Washington's streets cheered Nixon as his motorcade made its way from the Capitol to the White House. But hundreds of antiwar protesters who did not believe Nixon would quickly end the conflict spoiled the proudest day of Nixon's life. Protesters mocked his campaign slogan "Nixon's the One" with signs that claimed "Nixon's the one ... the No. 1 War Criminal." They held other negative signs and chanted antiwar phrases, like "four more years of death," because they believed Nixon would continue the war. Protesters threw stones, trash, and smoke bombs at his motorcade.

The protesters, most of them college students, symbolized the most difficult problem Nixon faced as president. The way Nixon dealt with the war and how he reacted to anyone who criticized his handling of the conflict ignited a series of incidents that culminated in the Watergate break-in. H.R. Haldeman, one of Nixon's top aides, once summed up the connection between the Vietnam War and Watergate. He said, "Without the Vietnam War, there would have been no Watergate. Without a Vietnam War, Richard Nixon might have had the most successful presidency since [Democrat] Harry Truman's [from 1945 to 1952]. But the Vietnam war destroyed Nixon."[23]

The Vietnam War

The Vietnam War was part of the Cold War, the twentieth-century conflict between Communist nations and democratic ones, like the United States. In 1955 Communist North Vietnam started using military force to obtain control of South Vietnam. The United States had

been providing military aid in the form of weapons and funds to South Vietnam since it had been created and in 1959 it began sending soldiers to train South Vietnam's army to better defend itself. By 1963 the United States had sixteen thousand soldiers in South Vietnam. When Lyndon B. Johnson became president after John F. Kennedy's assassination on November 22, 1963, he began sending many more soldiers there because South Vietnam was losing the conflict. By 1968 the number of Americans fighting there totaled 530,000.

Nixon's handling of the Vietnam War earned him harsh criticism from antiwar demonstrators.

Many Americans became angry because so many U.S. soldiers were being killed and wounded in a far-off war. They also resented the draft, a law that allowed the federal government to force men to join the armed forces. People began staging antiwar demonstrations to demand that the United States quit fighting; many protests involved violence, both by demonstrators and police, who tried to stop or control the events. Many citizens, however, supported the war, because they believed the nation needed to fight communism. The result was political turmoil and division throughout the nation.

After Nixon was elected, he still refused to explain how he would end the war. In May 1969 he told the nation that "peace cannot be achieved overnight, cannot be settled in a single stroke."[24] Nixon did not predict a quick resolution of the conflict, because he was determined to defeat the Communists and avoid becoming the first president to lose a war.

In June 1969 Nixon reduced the number of troops in Vietnam by about

The Longest War in U.S. History

The United States participated in the Vietnam War from 1959 until April 30, 1975, when its last soldiers left South Vietnam. The war lasted longer than any other in U.S. history. The Vietnam War is also known as the Second Indochina War, because it was part of an even longer military conflict. In the mid-nineteenth century, France used its superior military and economic strength to make Cambodia, Laos, and Vietnam its colonies. France called the area Indochina, and it governed the countries, sometimes brutally, and benefited economically from their natural resources. In the twentieth century, the Vietnamese began demanding the right to rule themselves. Ho Chi Minh, a Communist, created the League for the Independence of Vietnam, which is better known as the Viet Minh. After World War II, the Viet Minh began a war with France for Vietnam's independence. After the Viet Minh triumphed in 1954, the United Nations (UN) divided Vietnam in half to create North Vietnam and South Vietnam because there was also battle for political control between Ho Chi Minh's Communists and Vietnamese who wanted a democratic nation. The UN said it would hold a national election in 1956 to unify Vietnam. When no elections were held because South Vietnam feared North Vietnamese leader Ho Chi Minh would be elected to head the country, Communist North Vietnam began a military campaign to obtain control of all Vietnam. In 1959 the United States began helping South Vietnam as part of its global Cold War battle against communism.

sixty-nine thousand to calm the nation's growing antiwar sentiment. But even as Nixon was bringing soldiers home, he was expanding the war to neighboring Cambodia. Cambodia was officially neutral in the conflict, but on March 15 Nixon ordered bombing attacks on trails in Cambodia that the North Vietnamese were using to get supplies to their soldiers in South Vietnam. The bombings remained secret until May 9 when the *New York Times* published a story about them. The front-page story increased antiwar sentiment against Nixon. The story also made Nixon so furious that he began to use illegal tactics to fight his critics and opponents.

The Plumbers

An angry Nixon told his aides, "Find out who leaked it [the bombing story], and fire him!"[25] He ordered the Federal Bureau of Investigation (FBI) to place wiretaps on the telephones of officials who he suspected of giving the secret information to the *New York Times* and on the telephones of journalists who may have received the information.

Nixon continued using telephone wiretaps, both legally and illegally, for the rest of his presidency to identify people who leaked news items that hurt him or to discover what his opponents were doing. This effort increased dramatically after the *New York Times* began printing a top-secret government report on June 13, 1971. The report, known as the Pentagon Papers, details how the United States became involved in the Vietnam War and how it had slowly

escalated its participation in the conflict. The report increased antiwar sentiment, and a national Gallup poll soon showed that for the first time, a majority of Americans wanted to end U.S. participation in the war.

The president had Attorney General John Mitchell file a lawsuit to stop the *New York Times* from publishing the report. Claiming that its publication threatened national security, Mitchell was able to obtain a restraining order to stop the *Times* from printing it. So the *Times* gave the documents to other newspapers, and they published them. On June 30 the U.S. Supreme Court, in a ruling that vindicated freedom of the press, said the report could be printed because it did not threaten national security.

Nixon was so furious that he demanded an end to all leaks. "I don't give a damn how it's done, do whatever has to be done to stop these leaks and prevent further unauthorized disclosures," Nixon told White House staff members. "I want it done. Whatever the cost."[26] To do this, his staff created the White House Special Investigations Unit, which became known as the Plumbers because its job was to stop "leaks." Nixon aide John Ehrlichman oversaw the activities of this group, which included E. Howard Hunt and G. Gordon Liddy, who would later become central figures in the Watergate burglary.

The Plumbers learned that former Defense Department analyst Daniel Ellsberg, who now opposed the war, had given the Pentagon Papers to the *New York Times*. On July 27, the FBI reported to White House aides that Ellsberg had

Daniel Ellsberg, center, testifying before an unofficial House panel about the Pentagon Papers, was targeted by the Nixon Administration for leaking the papers to the press.

been treated by Lewis Fielding, a Los Angeles psychiatrist. Liddy and Hunt suggested the Plumbers break into Fielding's office to get Ellsberg's medical records, which might have information that could be used to tarnish Ellsberg's reputation. Ehrlichman discussed the suggestion with Nixon, who verbally approved it. Ehrlichman told the Plumbers to perform the burglary. But in a written memo, he warned them it could only be "done under your assurance that it is not traceable."[27] Ehrlichman meant that they could only perform the burglary if they were certain not to leave evidence connecting the illegal act to Nixon.

The Plumbers burglarized Fielding's office on September 2 but failed to find any negative information about Ellsberg. The burglary was similar to the one that would be repeated a year later at Watergate.

War and Protests Continue

Nixon is credited with some successes in his first term. On September 5, 1969, the U.S. Supreme Court ordered Mississippi to immediately begin desegregating schools. The Nixon administration enforced the ruling in Mississippi and neighboring states, and by the fall of 1970, 2 million southern black children were attending integrated schools. In foreign affairs Nixon is hailed for his February 1972 trip to the People's Republic of China to meet Communist leader Mao Zedong. The trip opened a new era of diplomacy between the two nations, which two decades earlier had fought each other in the Korean War.

Despite his accomplishments, many Americans were unhappy with Nixon, because he had failed to end the Vietnam War. Nixon had gradually reduced the number of soldiers fighting there through his policy of Vietnamization, which required South Vietnam to expand its army to do more fighting. And the United States was also conducting peace negotiations with North Vietnam, but they were proceeding slowly. However, at the same time Nixon was withdrawing troops and negotiating, he was increasing bombing attacks on North Vietnam and Cambodia.

On April 30, 1970, Nixon infuriated antiwar opponents anew when he announced on television that U.S. troops would enter Cambodia to attack North Vietnamese sanctuaries there. In his address Nixon said, "To protect our men who are in Vietnam and to guarantee the continued success of our withdrawal and Vietnamization programs, I have concluded that the time has come for action."[28] The expansion of the war into Cambodia ignited the most violent antiwar demonstrations the United States had seen yet. Most protests were on college campuses as students vented their anger over the war by destroying school property or rampaging through surrounding areas. Students even took control of campuses for brief periods until police began arresting them. Some protests were so bad that state governments called out the National Guard to police the violence.

At Kent State University in Kent, Ohio, students broke store windows in Kent and burned down a school building that housed a military training program. On May 4 the Ohio National Guard was trying to control about two thousand students at Kent State when nervous guardsmen, fearing for their own safety, opened fire on the protesters. The shots killed four students and wounded nine more. Two of the slain students—Allison Krause and Jeffrey Miller—were protesters, but Sandra Scheuer and William Knox Schroeder were not. They were killed while walking to class.

Nixon hated the antiwar protesters for opposing his policy. He issued a statement about the deaths that made him seem more upset by the violence the students had committed than the deaths. "This," Nixon said, "should remind us all once again that when dissent turns to violence it invites tragedy."[29] The president's callous reaction to the deaths of four students added to the anger of antiwar protesters, who called the shooting the "Kent State Massacre." The reaction to events at Kent State ignited a wave of violent protests at college campuses across the nation. Two more students were killed on May 14 at Jackson State College in Jackson, Mississippi, in a confrontation with local and state police. Eventually, nearly five hundred colleges and universities ended their spring semesters early because of protests, which in some cases escalated into full-scale riots.

By 1970, however, college students were not the only ones protesting the Vietnam War, and the war became the focus of Nixon's bid to win a second term as president.

Nixon's harsh response to the deaths of four Kent State students during an antiwar demonstration added to his unpopularity with those opposed to the war.

The 1972 Presidential Election

By 1972 many Democratic elected officials and even a few Republicans had begun to believe the United States should quit fighting the Vietnam War, because there was no way to stop North Vietnam from winning. One of the most vocal national officials to oppose the war was U.S. senator George McGovern of South Dakota. When McGovern realized Nixon was still trying to win the war and not end it, he was the first senator to openly criticize Nixon for failing to fulfill his promise to end the conflict. In a speech on March 17, 1969, only a few months after Nixon was sworn in as president, McGovern said, "There is no more time for considering 'military options,' no more time for 'improving the bargaining position [with North Vietnam].' I believe the only acceptable objective now is an immediate end to the killing."[30]

In response to the Cambodia invasion, McGovern and Republican senator Mark Hatfield of Oregon introduced a bill to Congress in May 1970 to cut off funding for military operations in Cambodia and Laos. The U.S. military had also begun pursuing Communist soldiers into Laos, which also bordered South Vietnam. The bill also required the withdrawal of all U.S. soldiers by the end of 1971. McGovern bitterly scolded his fellow senators when they rejected the measure. He claimed they had a moral responsibility for the deaths of U.S. soldiers in the war. McGovern said, "Every Senator in this chamber is partly responsible for sending 50,000 young Americans to an early grave. This chamber reeks of blood."[31]

McGovern's stature for opposing the war rose despite his failure to pass the measure. His strong antiwar credentials helped him win the 1972 Democratic nomination for president, which meant he would face Nixon in the election.

Planning the Break-in

To raise money and manage his second bid for the presidency, Nixon created the Committee to Re-elect the President; its initials were CRP, but some people, mainly political foes, referred to it as "CREEP." The committee was headed by John Mitchell, who had resigned as attorney general to run his friend's campaign. Despite rising antiwar sentiment, Nixon was heavily favored to beat McGovern because many people still supported the war, which was the election's overriding issue. To ensure Nixon would win, Mitchell set aside $250,000 to pay for finding out the Democratic Party's campaign plans.

The White House Plumbers was disbanded in the fall of 1971. However, G. Gordon Liddy and E. Howard Hunt, who had been involved in the burglary of Daniel Ellsberg's psychiatrist's office, were still working for the White House and the CRP. They proposed Operation GEMSTONE, a secret plan to spy on and disrupt the Democratic presidential campaign to make sure Nixon would win. One of their

Operation Gemstone

Burglarizing Democratic National Committee offices was not the only illegal act G. Gordon Liddy recommended to help President Richard M. Nixon win reelection. In a meeting with Attorney General John Mitchell on January 27, 1972, Liddy outlined several other illegal political intelligence actions in what he called Operation GEMSTONE. In his book, *The Arrogance of Power*, author Anthony Summers writes,

> One part of the operation, code named DIAMOND, outlined methods of dealing with "urban guerrillas" expected to disrupt the Republican convention. They were to be identified in advance, kidnapped, drugged, and held incommunicado in Mexico until after the convention. Another component, RUBY, was a scheme to infiltrate spies into the Democratic camp. COAL was designed to feed money clandestinely to black [Democratic] Congresswoman Shirley Chisolm [and] EMERALD called for a pursuit plane to bug radiotelephone transmissions from aircraft carrying the Democratic candidate. [Liddy] went on to brief his colleagues on OPAL, for clandestine entries to place bugs; TOPAZ, for photographing documents; and GARNET, for mountain sham pro-Democratic demonstrations carried out in a way that would repel voters rather than attract them. There was also TURQUOISE, which would undertake sabotage at the Democratic convention.

Quoted in Anthony Summers, *The Arrogance of Power: The Secret World of Richard Nixon*. New York: Viking, 2000, p. 324.

suggestions was to break into the offices of the Democratic National Committee (DNC), which was running McGovern's campaign. Liddy and Hunt wanted to place wiretaps on telephone lines and photograph documents to obtain information that would help Nixon beat McGovern. Their main target was the office of DNC chairman Lawrence O'Brien.

On March 30, 1972, Mitchell discussed the Watergate break-in with Jeb Magruder, a former presidential assistant working for CRP, and presidential assistant Frederick C. LaRue, one of many White House aides helping to reelect Nixon. Mitchell expressed doubt that the break-in would work. "How do we know that these guys know what they're doing?"[32] he asked. Despite his reservations, Mitchell approved the plan that day.

In late April, Magruder met with Liddy and told him to go ahead with the burglary. "We want to know whatever's said in his office, just as if it were here,

John Mitchell resigned his post as attorney general in order to run Nixon's presidential campaign. He authorized the Watergate break-in.

what goes on in this office," he instructed Liddy. "Get in there as soon as you can, Gordon; it's important."[33] Magruder also told Liddy to photograph campaign documents, especially lists of people who had donated money to McGovern's campaign.

The Watergate

Liddy and Hunt recruited a break-in team and began preparing for the illegal act on May 22, the same day Nixon arrived in Moscow for a meeting with leaders of the Soviet Union. The burglars began by visiting Watergate, a large complex of six buildings, to gather information about its physical layout. James W. McCord Jr., a former Central Intelligence Agency (CIA) agent now working for CRP, rented room 419 in the Howard Johnson Motor Inn opposite Watergate. The room served as a meeting place for the team and would be a listening post for the wiretaps. Alfred Baldwin was stationed in the room to monitor the taps. Liddy, Hunt, and four others who helped McCord in the break-in—Bernard L. Barker, Frank A. Sturgis, Eugenio R. Martinez, and Virgilio R. Gonzalez—also rented rooms in the Watergate Hotel.

The burglars tried unsuccessfully for two nights to get into the DNC offices. On May 26 they failed to get from the Watergate Hotel to the adjoining office building before the security system activated at 11 P.M. in the corridor connecting the two halves of the complex. The next night they gained entry directly to the office building, but could not open the locked doors of the DNC offices. The team finally succeeded in breaking in on May 28, placing two telephone bugs and photographing documents. Liddy and Hunt participated in the break-in by monitoring the activities of the burglars from the Watergate hotel rooms via walkie-talkies.

For the next few weeks, team members monitored conversations in the DNC offices from the Howard Johnson hotel room across the street. However, one bug was not working, and the second was not picking up important information, because the team failed to place it in O'Brien's office. Magruder was unhappy with the surveillance, and on June 12 he told Liddy to send the team back to fix the problems. He also wanted more photographs of documents. "Take all the men, all the cameras you need,"[34] he told Liddy. Liddy said Magruder especially wanted data from O'Brien's office about negative information the Democrats had on Nixon that they planned to use during the campaign.

"Don't Shoot, We Give Up."

On Saturday, June 17, 1972, Liddy and Hunt again remained in the Watergate hotel rooms, while McCord, Barker, Gonzalez, Martinez, and Sturgis broke into the DNC offices again. McCord had earlier taped open the lock on a garage-level door leading to a stairwell to the DNC offices, but when the team got to that door, the tape was gone. Gonzalez, a locksmith, then opened the door and several other locked doors and taped

The Arrest

Virgilio R. Gonzalez, James W. McCord Jr., Bernard L. Barker, Frank A. Sturgis, and Eugenio R. Martinez broke into the Democratic National Committee (DNC) offices on June 17, 1972. In his book *Watergate: The Corruption of American Politics and the Fall of Richard Nixon*, historian Fred Emery describes how the burglars were arrested:

> Inside the DNC the team had been moving toward its tasks: Gonzalez to open the glass door to [DNC chairman Lawrence] O'Brien's suite, McCord accompanying Barker to the file area, Sturgis and Martinez were on guard at the door. McCord says he picked up some college press credential forms for the Democratic convention. [Then] Sturgis arrived saying somebody was coming. A light went on and they heard shouts of "Come out, police!" The team's exit was barred; they had no alternative but to crouch down, hoping not to be seen. McCord has said that were the police search less thorough, they might have escaped detection. But the police searched each cubicle in the DNC in turn. Officer [John] Barrett was the first to spot an arm move behind the glass [partition] and shouted, "Hold it. Come out." Sergeant [Paul] Leeper, who had also drawn his revolver, jumped onto a desk, looked over the partition, and saw five men. They were raising their hands, which he remembered were covered with blue rubber gloves. Some were trying to remove the gloves. At this point, [G. Gordon] Liddy says, came the first and last transmission, a whisper, from the entry team: "They got us."

Fred Emery, *Watergate: The Corruption of American Politics and the Fall of Richard Nixon*. New York: Random House, 1994, p. 135.

them to stay open. The five then proceeded to the DNC offices and began their work.

While the break-in was underway, security guard Frank Wills discovered some of the taped-open doors. After asking a superior what to do, Wills called police at 1:47 A.M. to report a suspected break-in. Responding to the call were three members of a tactical unit dressed in civilian clothes—Sergeant Paul Leeper and Officers John Barrett and Carl Shoffler. The trio began a floor-by-floor search of the office building and eventually found the burglars. When the policemen entered the DNC offices, the burglars tried to hide. But Barrett spotted one of the five men and shouted,

Evidence from the Watergate break-in, including lights and bugging equipment. The sophisticated equipment used by the Watergate burglars was a tip-off to law enforcement that this was no ordinary break-in.

"Hands up."[35] After Barrett and Shoffler discovered the men crouched down in a cubicle, the burglars raised their hands and one reportedly said "Don't shoot, we give up."[36]

The three policemen were surprised by the five burglars, because they did not seem like typical burglars. They were wearing businesses suits and rubber gloves. They also had equipment not normally found on burglars—listening devices, film and two cameras, three pen-size tear-gas guns, a walkie-talkie, and almost twenty-three hundred dollars in cash.

Police took them to jail and charged them with felonious burglary and possession of implements of crime—the burglary tools they used to open doors—in what at first seemed to be a bizarre, but minor burglary. Wills was hailed as a hero for discovering the break-in. "I did the right thing," said Wills. "I was just doing my job."[37]

No one that night could have predicted the outcome of Wills having done his job properly. The arrests would explode into the biggest political scandal in U.S. history and lead to the downfall of a president.

Chapter Three

The Cover-Up

On Sunday, June 18, 1972, the day after the burglary, President Richard M. Nixon was reading the *Miami Herald* newspaper in Key Biscayne, Florida, when he read about the break-in at the Democratic National Committee (DNC) offices. In his memoirs Nixon writes that he was stunned by the incident, and it seemed so bizarre to him that he believed someone must have been playing a practical joke on the Democrats. But later that day, Nixon told H.R. "Bob" Haldeman, his White House chief of staff, that he was worried someone connected with his reelection campaign might have been involved in it. But Nixon told Haldeman that even if that was true, he did not think it would hurt his chances to be re-elected. He said, "It has to be some crazies over at CRP [Committee to Re-elect the President], Bob. That's what it was. And what does it matter? The American people will see it for what it was: a political prank."[38]

Nixon knew about some of the past illegal activities his staffers committed, including the 1971 burglary of the office of Daniel Ellsberg's psychiatrist. However, there is no evidence he knew about the Watergate burglary before it happened. On Monday Press Secretary Ron Ziegler downplayed the incident's importance in his daily meeting with reporters. In response to a question about the break-in, Ziegler said, "It's a third-rate burglary attempt [and] nothing the president would be involved with, obviously."[39] Most historians believe Nixon advised Ziegler on what to say about Watergate because of his fear that there might be a connection to his campaign.

Ziegler's comment became one of the most famous involving Watergate. Many people point to Ziegler's attempt to dismiss the burglary as unimportant as the beginning of Nixon's attempt to cover it up. However, the men directly

Ron Ziegler, Nixon's press secretary, famously described Watergate as a "third-rate burglary."

involved in the burglary and other Nixon staffers had already begun that process. Unfortunately for Nixon, so had the attempts by reporters to investigate Watergate.

"I'll Probably Be Going to Jail"

When the burglars were arrested, G. Gordon Liddy and E. Howard Hunt realized they could be traced to the Watergate hotel rooms they had rented. Liddy and Hunt frantically packed up electronic equipment and other incriminating evidence and quickly left the Watergate. Alfred Baldwin was in the Howard Johnson room that served as a

listening post for the telephone taps. He also fled with electronic equipment and other evidence that could be linked to the burglary.

Liddy went home. When his wife woke up about 3 A.M. as he was going to bed, Liddy told her, "There was trouble. Some people got caught. I'll probably be going to jail."[40] Hunt went to the White House, where he had an office because he was working for Nixon's campaign. Hunt put the electronic equipment, an address book, and a notebook with information on his CRP activities into a safe. Hunt then called attorney Douglas Caddy and asked him to represent the men who had been

Watergate conspirator James McCord demonstrates to the Senate Watergate committee in 1973 bugging equipment used in the telephones at Democratic headquarters.

arrested—James W. McCord Jr., Bernard L. Barker, Virgilio R. Gonzalez, Eugenio R. Martinez, and Frank A. Sturgis.

The burglars, meanwhile, were obstructing the investigation by giving police false identities, something they had been instructed to do if arrested. McCord and Sturgis were even carrying fake identification they had from their time with the Central Intelligence Agency (CIA). The attempts to mislead authorities failed because police identified them by their fingerprints.

While the five were waiting to be charged, Liddy began destroying evidence connecting the burglary to the White House. After a few hours of sleep, Liddy got up at 7 A.M. and tried to call CRP staffer Jeb Magruder. When he learned Magruder was in Los Angeles, California, with John Mitchell, where it was only 4 A.M., he decided to talk to him about the botched burglary later. Liddy drove to the CRP offices and used a shredder to destroy Operation GEMSTONE documents and other

Nixon Defends Bugging

In *The Memoirs of Richard Nixon*, the former president writes that he had not believed bugging Democratic telephones would upset people, because it was a common practice in politics. Many people believe Nixon used his memoirs to try to minimize the act that ultimately led to his resignation from office. Nixon writes,

> My reaction to the Watergate break-in was completely pragmatic. If it was also cynical, it was a cynicism born of experience. I had been in politics too long, and seen everything from dirty tricks to vote fraud. I could not muster much moral outrage over a political bugging. [Democratic Party chairman] Larry O'Brien might affect astonishment and horror, but he knew as well as I did that political bugging had been around nearly since the invention of the wiretap. As recently as 1970 a former member of [Democrat] Adlai Stevenson's campaign staff had publicly stated that he had tapped the [John F.] Kennedy organization's phone lines at the 1960 Democratic convention. Lyndon Johnson felt that the Kennedy organization had him tapped [and] bugging experts told the *Washington Post* right after the Watergate break-in that the practice "has not been uncommon in elections past ... it is particularly common for candidates of the same party to bug one another."

Richard M. Nixon, *The Memoirs of Richard Nixon*. New York: Grosset and Dunlap, 1978, pp. 628–629.

evidence linking the burglary to the president's campaign. He even shredded one hundred dollar bills which were part of thousands of dollars the campaign had given him to fund GEMSTONE because he feared the bills could be traced to the CRP's financial records through their serial numbers. Liddy then went to the White House and called Magruder. He used a White House telephone to make the call because it was a secure line that could not be electronically tapped.

Magruder was dismayed that the burglars had been arrested. Magruder told Mitchell that his main concern was that the burglars could be linked to the CRP. That also concerned Mitchell, who was especially worried about McCord, who worked directly for the campaign. Mitchell had an aide call Attorney General Richard Kleindienst and order him to get McCord out of jail before his identity was discovered. When Kleindienst refused, Magruder, Mitchell, and White House aide Fred LaRue continued discussing their options in handling the situation. It was during this discussion that Magruder began to understand that the burglary was so serious that they needed to protect the president by concealing White House involvement in it. He said, "I realized that this was not just hard-nosed politics, this was a crime that could destroy us all. The cover-up, thus, was immediate and automatic; no one ever considered that there would *not* be a cover-up. It seemed inconceivable that with our political power we could not erase this mistake we had made."[41]

It was, however, too late to stop the incident from being made public. The burglars were already being formally charged in court with the crime they had committed.

Front-Page News

The burglars were arraigned at 3:30 P.M. on Saturday, June 17 before Judge James A. Belsen. When Belsen asked the men their professions, one said they were dedicated to fighting communism and several others agreed with that description. McCord said he worked as a security consultant and had recently retired from government service. When Belsen asked "Where in government?" McCord replied softly "CIA."[42]

McCord had tried to speak in a whisper so one else in the courtroom would hear him, but *Washington Post* reporter Bob Woodward understood the response. Realizing it was significant that a former government spy was involved in a break-in, Woodward took a cab back to his office to make sure that information was added to the story about the burglary before the 6:30 P.M. deadline for the next day's edition of the newspaper. On Sunday, June 18, the *Washington Post* carried a front-page story on the burglary. Eight reporters, including Woodward and Carl Bernstein, had contributed facts to the story. Under the headline "5 Held in Plot to Bug Democrats' Office Here," its opening paragraph read, "Five men, one of whom said he is a former employee of the Central Intelligence Agency, were arrested at 2:30 A.M. yesterday in what authorities described as an elaborate plot to bug the offices of the Democratic National Committee here."[43]

In just a few hours, the reporters had gathered key facts about the burglars, including that four were exiles from Cuba and that Sturgis had helped train Cuban exiles for the failed 1961 Bay of Pigs invasion to overthrow Communist leader Fidel Castro. Like most burglars, they had tools to pick locks. But the story noted that unlike most burglars, they were wearing rubber gloves to conceal their fingerprints, had sophisticated electronic equipment, and carried almost twenty-three hundred dollars in cash, most of it in one hundred dollar bills with consecutive serial numbers. The five men were charged with felony burglary and possession of implements of crime. Bail was set at fifty thousand dollars each for four of them and thirty thousand dollars for McCord; his bail was lower because he lived locally and was considered less of a risk to flee the area.

The fact that McCord was a former government spy gave the incident ominous overtones. In a follow-up story later that Sunday, the Associated Press news agency reported that McCord was the security coordinator for Nixon's reelection campaign. The connection to the CRP made the burglary a much bigger story, because it now directly involved the president. The *Post* assigned Woodward and Bernstein to continue investigating the burglary full time because of the political ramifications it now had for the upcoming presidential election.

But while reporters like Woodward and Bernstein were scrambling to uncover facts about the burglary, CRP and White House staff members were working to keep them buried.

Covering Up Watergate

In California, Mitchell gave reporters a written statement about the burglary on Monday, June 19. The statement said that McCord had installed security systems for the campaign, but that the CRP had not ordered McCord to perform the burglary. It also said, "We want to emphasize that this man and the other people involved were not operating either on our behalf or with our consent. I am surprised and dismayed at these reports."[44]

Mitchell's lie about the CRP not ordering McCord to perform the burglary is just one example of how people connected to the president were trying to conceal evidence of their involvement in the burglary. Magruder destroyed GEMSTONE files he had at his home. John W. Dean III, who advised Nixon on legal matters, went through the contents of Hunt's White House safe. Wearing rubber gloves to avoid leaving fingerprints, Dean removed documents concerning the burglary and other illegal activities connected to the CRP.

No one is sure exactly when or how Nixon learned that his reelection campaign had planned and carried out the burglary, but it was probably the day after it occurred. The news frightened Nixon, who feared that the Federal Bureau of Investigation (FBI) would

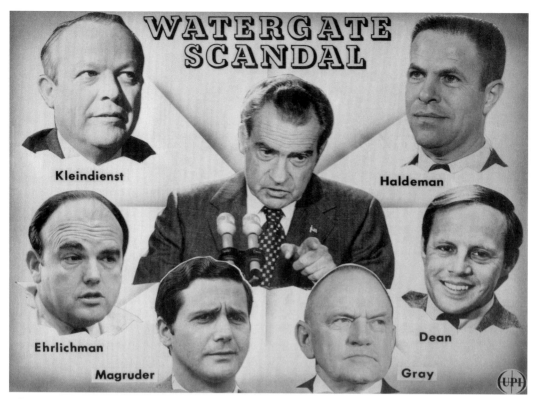

The major figures of the Watergate scandal surrounding Richard Nixon, clockwise from the top: H.R. Haldeman, John W. Dean, L. Patrick Gray, Jeb Magruder, John D. Ehrlichman, and Richard Kleindienst.

discover the connection. Mitchell was also concerned that the nation's top law enforcement agency could discover the CRP's involvement, and he devised a plan to make the FBI quit probing Watergate. Mitchell wanted the White House to persuade deputy CIA director Vernon Walters to ask acting FBI director L. Patrick Gray to stop investigating Watergate. The FBI handles domestic crime and security threats to the nation, while the CIA focuses on foreign threats to the United States. The two federal agencies have a working agreement to stay out of each other's affairs when their interests overlap. Because

four of the burglars were Cuban, Mitchell wanted Walters to tell Gray that the incident involved Cuba, which would make it a CIA responsibility.

Mitchell did not tell the president directly about his plan. But on June 23, Haldeman had several conversations in the White House with Nixon about Mitchell's suggestion on how to handle the FBI. Nixon liked the plan and even suggested some details to make the CIA explanation to the FBI more believable. Nixon said that the Bay of Pigs—the failed attempt by Cuban exiles supported by the U.S. government to invade

Communist Cuba in 1961—could be used to get the FBI to quit investigating Watergate. Nixon believed the FBI would end its investigation if it thought Watergate involved some aspect of the invasion the government did not want revealed publicly. Nixon told Haldeman, "[Say to the CIA that] the President's belief is that this is going to open the whole Bay of Pigs thing up again [and] that they [the CIA] should call the FBI in and say that we wish for the country [not to] go any further into this case."[45]

This is believed to be the first time Nixon took an active part in the cover-up of White House involvement in Watergate. One reason Nixon wanted the FBI investigation stopped was that the agency was close to discovering that the cash the burglars had was from the CRP. Walters was contacted later that day, and he called Gray. However, the effort to stop the FBI failed, because the Watergate investigation was being conducted by Earl Silbert, a U.S. attorney for the District of Columbia.

Thus FBI agents, on Silbert's orders, continued investigating the burglary and the men who had committed it. So did Woodward and Bernstein, who were digging up key facts about White House involvement in Watergate.

Liddy Destroys Evidence

Only hours after the Watergate break-in, G. Gordon Liddy went to the offices of the Committee to Re-elect the President (CRP) to destroy documents concerning the burglary and other illegal activities he was involved in because he knew the documents would implicate him. In his book, *Will*, Liddy explains how he destroyed evidence:

The small [paper] shredder was too slow. I had confidence in my men [the five men already arrested], but I had to act on the assumption that it was just a matter of time before the FBI [Federal Bureau of Investigation] was coming to my office with a search warrant. I knew that there was a huge, high-capacity shredder somewhere in the committee complex, but I didn't know where. I sought out the man who would know, Rob Odle, and he directed me to it and showed me how to operate it. I didn't like Odle's shredder. It cut paper into strips the size of confetti, not threads. [The] most sensitive [documents] would have to go into the small, slow, few-sheets-at-a-time high-security model near my office.

G. Gordon Liddy, *Will*. New York: St. Martin's, 1980, p. 249.

Woodward and Bernstein Investigate

Although Woodward reported about McCord's CIA past in his newspaper's first Watergate story, he made the mistake of not checking out McCord's background more thoroughly. If he had, he would have learned that McCord was a CRP employee. The Associated Press (AP), however, did discover it, and the AP is credited with the "scoop"—being the first to report the information. Woodward redeemed himself the next day by discovering that E. Howard Hunt was connected to the burglary. Woodward learned from another reporter that references to a "Mr. Howard" and a "Mr. H.H." appeared in notebooks the burglars had when they were arrested.

Woodward was able to identify the man as Hunt. He telephoned the White House to see if Hunt worked there. He was surprised to learn that Hunt was a consultant to Charles Colson, who handled political matters for Nixon, including his campaign.

Woodward immediately called Hunt, who refused to comment. Woodward then telephoned Ken W. Clawson, a former *Washington Post* reporter who was the White House deputy director of communications. Clawson admitted that Hunt had done some security work for Colson but was no longer employed by the White House. Clawson then claimed, "[No one] at the White House had any knowledge of, or participation in, this deplorable incident at the Democratic National

Democratic National Committee chairman Lawrence O'Brien believed that the White House was responsible for the Watergate break-in and called for a full investigation.

Woodstein

Although reporters for many newspapers investigated Watergate, Bob Woodward and Carl Bernstein of the *Washington Post* uncovered the most important facts about the burglary and the attempted cover-up. Because they shared a byline for their Watergate stories, they were nicknamed "Woodstein." The partnership, however, was not always a smooth one. In the book, *All the President's Men* written by Woodward and Bernstein, they explain how they began to work as a team:

> Gradually, Bernstein's and Woodward's mutual distrust and suspicion diminished. They realized the advantage of working together, particularly because their temperaments were so dissimilar. The breadth of the story, the inherent risks and the need for caution all argued for at least two reporters working on it. By dividing the work and pooling their information, they increased their contacts. [To] those who sat nearby in the [*Post*] newsroom, it was obvious that Woodstein was not always a smoothly operating piece of journalistic machinery. The two fought, often openly. Sometimes they battled for fifteen minutes over a word or sentence. Nuances were critically important; the emphasis had to be just right. The search for the journalistic mean was frequently conducted at full volume, and it was not uncommon to see one stalk away from the other's desk. Sooner or later, however (usually later), the story was hammered out.

Quoted in Carl Bernstein and Bob Woodward, *All the President's Men*. New York: Simon and Schuster, 1974, pp. 49–50.

Committee."[46] Woodward thought the comment was suspicious because Clawson volunteered it without being asked if there was a White House connection. Woodward's next story about Watergate on June 20 described what he had learned, establishing another key link between the burglars and the White House.

Carl Bernstein discovered that a twenty-five-thousand-dollar check given to the CRP by a political donor had been deposited in Bernard L. Barker's Florida bank account, and his story about it was published August 1. CRP officials claimed they did not know how the money got into Barker's account. However, the financial connection between the CRP and Barker made more people suspect the burglary had been ordered by campaign or White House officials.

The DNC Sues

From the beginning, Democrats believed the CRP and the White House were responsible for the break-in. On June 20 Democratic National Committee (DNC) chairman Lawrence O'Brien filed a $1-million lawsuit against the CRP for invasion of privacy and violation of the party's civil rights. O'Brien claimed the burglary had been politically motivated by the Republicans. He said, "Continuing disclosures in the wake of Saturday's bugging incident at the DNC raise the ugliest questions about the integrity of the political process that I have encountered in a quarter century of political activity."[47] O'Brien called for a full investigation of the burglary to punish those responsible for it.

Despite continuing news stories linking the White House to Watergate, Nixon remained far ahead of Senator George McGovern in his bid for reelection. It seemed that the nation did not care about the burglary.

A Landslide Victory

McGovern tried to capitalize on Watergate by blaming his Republican opponent. He called Watergate "a moral and Constitutional crisis of unprecedented dimensions" and claimed that "the whole ugly mess of corruption, of sabotage, of wiretapping [belonged] squarely in the lap of Richard Nixon."[48] O'Brien and other well-known Democrats also tried to make voters angry about Watergate. Most Americans, however, were slow to consider it a major issue in the campaign.

The public apathy toward the burglary did not surprise Nixon. On June 21,

just a few days after the burglary, the president was talking with Haldeman about how Watergate would affect his campaign. Nixon said he did not think it would hurt his reelection chances because most people would ignore it. He said,

> The reaction is going to be primarily [by political figures in] Washington and not the country [average citizens], because I think the country doesn't give much [concern] about it. [Most] people around the country think that this is routine, that everybody's trying to bug everybody else, it's politics. That's my view.[49]

Nixon's belief that most Americans would consider the burglary just another example of how the two parties played tricks on each other was true in the months after the burglary. Thus, Nixon was able to retain his substantial lead over McGovern in election polls despite a continuing flow of stories connecting Watergate to his campaign. The lack of public interest so emboldened Nixon that in August he claimed "no one in this administration, presently employed, was involved in this very bizarre incident."[50] That was a lie because many people connected to the burglary were still on his White House and campaign staffs.

Many people believe Nixon would have lost the election if voters had known he was concealing the truth from them and government officials. Because they did not, they elected him to a second term. In fact, Nixon defeated McGovern in one of the largest landslides in U.S. political history. Nixon won 60.7 percent of the votes and captured every state except South Dakota, McGovern's home state. Minor outrage over the Watergate scandal and Nixon's failure to end the Vietnam War, however, resulted in more Democrats being elected to Congress, where they already held substantial majorities in both the House and Senate.

Nixon Victorious But Sad

The victory was a tremendous boost for Nixon, who had worried for months that Watergate could mean his defeat. But in his memoirs, Nixon reveals that his elation over winning was tempered by several factors, including his continuing concern about Watergate. He writes,

I am at a loss to explain the melancholy that settled over me on that victorious night. . . . To some extent the marring effects of Watergate may have played a part, to some extent our [Republican] failure to win [control of] Congress, and to a greater extent the fact that we had not yet been able to end the war in Vietnam.[51]

Nixon, shown taking the Presidential oath of office in January 1973, won a second term as president despite the ongoing Watergate scandal.

All three factors in the next two years would combine to make Nixon the first president to resign from office. Anger over the war's continuation would make Nixon less popular. New revelations about the Watergate burglary and his administration's attempt to conceal it would lead to new investigations by Congress. And solid Democratic majorities in Congress would allow the Democrats to force Nixon to reveal the truth about what happened and begin proceedings to impeach him.

Chapter Four

A President Under Siege

When Richard M. Nixon was elected in 1968, he was filled with pride at being president. Not long afterward, Nixon was talking to a Florida banker and political supporter he had known for years. When the banker called him by his first name (which was Dick, a common nickname for Richard), Nixon became angry and lashed out at him, saying, "Don't you dare call me Dick. I am the president of the United States. When you speak to me you call me Mr. President."[52] Nixon believed he deserved the respect that goes with the title of "president" because the president of the United States wields more power than any leader of any nation in the world.

Nixon's overwhelming reelection victory in 1972 made him believe more firmly than ever that he was powerful and deserved such deference. But in the first few months of his second term, Nixon began to realize that his exalted status was in jeopardy because of the mounting political and legal furor over the Watergate burglary.

The Burglars Are Convicted

The first Watergate trial began on January 10, 1974, before federal judge John Sirica. Neither the defendants nor Nixon, who was worried that officials would learn his top aides had ordered the burglary, were happy that Sirica was the judge. He was a tough, hard-nosed judge, who had been nicknamed "Maximum John" because he usually gave criminals the maximum sentences the law allowed.

Gordon G. Liddy, E. Howard Hunt, James W. McCord Jr., Bernard L. Barker, Virgilio R. Gonzalez, Eugenio R. Martinez, and Frank A. Sturgis were charged with conspiracy, burglary, and wiretapping. Liddy and Hunt had been arrested and charged when new evidence proved they had been involved. In a pretrial

Judge John J. Sirica presided over the Watergate criminal case and pushed to get the truth.

hearing, Sirica said his goal was to find out all the facts of the burglary, including why it was done and who ordered it. He said the jury needed to know those facts to be able to decide if the defendants were guilty.

The trial did not fulfill Sirica's expectations because the defendants did not truthfully answer questions about what happened. The attempt to conceal the truth began on the trial's first day when Hunt changed his plea to guilty, which meant he would not have to answer as many questions. A few days later the four Cubans also pled guilty. Sirica then proceeded to try Liddy and McCord. As the trial progressed, Sirica did not think prosecuting attorneys were questioning the defendants thoroughly enough about the break-in, so Sirica asked his own questions.

Sirica wanted to know where the burglars got the thousands of dollars in one hundred dollar bills they had when they were arrested. The fact that the serial numbers on the bills were consecutively numbered was suspicious because it showed that the bills had come from the same source. When the judge asked Barker how he got his money, Barker said he had received the hundred dollar bills by mail in a blank envelope. Knowing Barker was not answering truthfully, Sirica bluntly responded, "I'm sorry. I don't believe you."[53]

Jurors heard testimony from sixty witnesses and viewed more than a hundred pieces of evidence. On January 30, jurors took less than ninety minutes to decide McCord and Liddy were guilty. Sirica set sentencing for March for all seven men. Despite the guilty verdicts, Sirica was unhappy the trial had failed to uncover more details about a crime with serious political overtones. Sirica told the defendants "I am still not satisfied that the pertinent facts that might be available—I say *might* be available—have been produced before an American jury."[54] Sirica also said he hoped future investigations would discover the truth about questions the trial had failed to answer.

The thought of future investigations frightened Nixon. But he had more important things to worry about, including ending the Vietnam War.

The Vietnam War Ends

The political issue that haunted Nixon's first term was the Vietnam War. For four years Nixon had tried to win the conflict while giving in to the demands of the American public to withdraw soldiers from the unpopular war. There were 534,000 U.S. soldiers in Vietnam when Nixon became president in January 1969. But Nixon's program of Vietnamization, which gradually forced South Vietnam to do more fighting, reduced the number of U.S. soldiers to fewer than 160,000 by 1971 and to about 23,000 by the end of 1972. But because Nixon was still trying to win the war, he had countered troop reductions with increased aerial bombing of combat areas and North Vietnam. Without massive numbers of U.S. soldiers, however, South Vietnam was losing the war.

Historians believe Nixon could have ended the war before the 1972 election.

Spiro Who?

In 1968 when Richard M. Nixon chose Maryland governor Spiro T. Agnew as his vice presidential running mate, many people were asking themselves "Spiro who?" because he was not very well-known. But Agnew became famous as vice president for two reasons: his witty attacks on reporters who criticized Nixon and his resignation in 1973 in connection with misconduct while in office. Agnew's biography on the U.S. Senate Web site explains Agnew's antimedia campaign:

> On November 13, 1969, Vice President Spiro Agnew became a household word when he vehemently denounced television news broadcasters as a biased "unelected elite" who subjected President Richard M. Nixon's

Nixon's vice president, Spiro Agnew, had to resign after being investigated for political misconduct.

> speeches to instant analysis. The president had a right to communicate directly with the people, Agnew asserted, without having his words "characterized through the prejudices of hostile critics." Agnew raised the possibility of greater government regulation of this "virtual monopoly," a suggestion that the veteran television newscaster Walter Cronkite took as "an implied threat to freedom of speech in this country." But Agnew's words rang true to [many people who backed Nixon]. From then until he resigned in 1973, Agnew remained an outspoken and controversial figure, who played traveling salesman for the administration. In this role, Spiro Agnew was both the creation of Richard Nixon and a reflection of his administration's siege mentality.

U.S. Senate, "Spiro T. Agnew, 39th Vice President (1969–1973)," U.S. Senate, www.senate.gov/artandhistory/history/common/generic/VP_Spiro_Agnew.htm.

They claim he did not because it would have hurt his chances for reelection by appearing to give in to demands by Senator George McGovern, his Democratic opponent, to end the war. After he was reelected, Nixon urged Henry Kissinger, his foreign affairs adviser who was negotiating with North Vietnam, to accept whatever terms the Communists wanted to end the fighting. "The war weariness has reached the point that it is just too much for us to carry on,"[55] Nixon told Kissinger of public opposition to the conflict. Kissinger returned to negotiations and quickly hammered out an agreement to end the war.

On the night of January 23, 1973, Nixon went on television to announce the war was over. "I have asked for this radio and television time tonight," Nixon said, "for the purpose of announcing that we today have concluded an agreement to end the war and bring peace with honor in Vietnam and Southeast Asia."[56] Nixon told war-weary Americans that a ceasefire would go into effect on January 27 and that the remaining 23,700 U.S. soldiers would come home within sixty days. In return North Vietnam agreed to release 651 prisoners of war.

Nixon never got much credit for ending the Vietnam War, because it took him more than four years to do it. He had been elected in 1968 partly because voters believed he had a plan to quickly end the conflict, and many people now criticized him for allowing it to continue as long as he did. In eleven years of fighting, 51,151 U.S. soldiers were killed in the Vietnam War, including almost 21,000 during his presidency. Nixon claimed he had achieved an honorable end to the war, but it was still the first one the United States did not win.

Even after the war ended, Nixon still faced many problems that continued to undermine confidence in his presidency. One of them involved criminal behavior by Vice President Spiro T. Agnew.

More Problems for Nixon

In 1968 Nixon chose Spiro T. Agnew, the governor of Maryland, as his running mate. As vice president, Agnew became valuable to Nixon for his ability to wittily attack the news media and other critics of the president. But in 1973, the U.S. Attorney's Office in Baltimore, Maryland, began investigating Agnew for political misconduct. In October officials charged Agnew with having accepted bribes totaling more than a hundred thousand dollars while serving as a Baltimore county executive, Maryland governor, and vice president.

The criminal charges were devastating for the Nixon administration, which was already under suspicion of illegal activities involving Watergate. Alexander Haig, a former army general, became Nixon's chief of staff in 1973. When Haig heard about Agnew, he thought to himself "God! We've got the worst of both worlds: a president who is on an impeachment trail, and a vice president who is guilty of felonies."[57]

On October 10, 1973, Agnew agreed to resign as vice president. It was part of a deal with prosecutors in which he only had to plead no contest to a single charge that he failed to report $29,500 in income received in 1967. In a no-contest plea, a defendant does not admit guilt but does not try to prove his innocence. Agnew was the second vice president to resign from office. John C. Calhoun was the first in 1832, but Agnew was the first to resign because of criminal charges. Two days later, Nixon named Representative Gerald R. Ford as his new vice president.

Nixon also struggled with a weak economy that suffered from unemployment and inflation. When Nixon resigned in 1974, unemployment and inflation were both higher than when he took office. Inflation skyrocketed in 1973 partly because of a shocking increase in the price of gasoline, which rose rapidly from a national average of 38.5 cents per gallon in May 1973 to 55.1 cents in June 1974.

The reason for the giant hike was the decision on October, 15, 1973, by Arab nations to limit oil production. The high gasoline prices hurt the U.S. economy, and the limited production also caused severe gasoline shortages; in some areas of the nation, drivers had to wait in long lines to fill their tanks and some stations ran out of gas. Arab nations had cut oil production to punish the United States because it helped Israel defend itself in October 1973 after Syria and Egypt attacked it. The United States sent weapons to Israel because it was the nation's most powerful ally in the Middle East. But when Kissinger told Nixon he should meet with reporters to explain the U.S. position on the war, Nixon told him, "You go ahead and tell [press secretary Ron] Ziegler whatever you want."[58] Ziegler's job was to speak on behalf of the president and he met daily with reporters. During the short-lived war which Israel won, Nixon allowed Kissinger, who was now his secretary of state, to make most of the major policy decisions. Nixon had given Kissinger that power because by then he was so busy defending himself from Watergate charges that he had little time to do anything else.

The Watergate Scandal Grows

Although many reporters were investigating Watergate, *Washington Post* reporters Bob Woodward and Carl Bernstein kept coming up with the biggest scoops. One reason for their success is that Woodward had a source in the federal government who was leaking important facts to him. William Mark Felt Sr., deputy director of the Federal Bureau of Investigation (FBI), was that source, and he leaked information to Woodward because he believed the public deserved to know that the Nixon administration was illegally covering up Watergate.

On January 25, 1973, Felt gave Woodward one of his most important leads. "Colson and Mitchell were behind the Watergate operation," Felt told him. "Everyone in the FBI is convinced, including Gray."[59] Felt was referring to White House aide Charles Colson; John N. Mitchell, the former attorney general and head of the Committee to Re-elect the President (CRP); and acting FBI

Former deputy director of the FBI, W. Mark Felt, was later revealed to be the secret source who helped Woodward and Bernstein break the Watergate scandal.

director L. Patrick Gray. Being able to report that Colson and Mitchell directed the break-in increased interest in the story, because they were closely associated with the president.

One of the most important breaks in uncovering Watergate came not from reporters but from one of the burglars. On March 20, 1974, McCord delivered a letter to Judge Sirica, who was scheduled to sentence him and the other Watergate burglars three days later. McCord admitted he and others had lied during the trial and failed to identify other people connected to the burglary. He even explained the reason they did that. He wrote, "There was political pressure applied to the defendants to plead guilty and remain silent."[60] The letter was dated March 19, Sirica's birthday, and he told an aide, "This is the best damned birthday present I've ever gotten. This is going to break the case wide open."[61] Sirica believed McCord's cooperation would allow federal officials to learn important new information about the burglary.

McCord hoped Judge Sirica would give him a lighter sentence if he cooperated with the investigation. On March 23, Sirica issued preliminary sentences for everyone but McCord that ranged between twenty and forty years in prison. Sirica then told the burglars he would reduce their sentences if they cooperated with government prosecutors investigating the burglary. On March 28, McCord told federal prosecutors that Liddy had told him the Watergate operation had been approved by Mitchell while he was still attorney general. In November Sirica rewarded McCord by giving him a sentence of only one to five years.

For the first time, one of the burglars and not a newspaper reporter had connected Watergate to one of Nixon's cabinet members and closest friends. The fallout from that testimony and other new facts authorities were uncovering forced Nixon to work harder than ever to avoid being destroyed politically.

The Cover-up Grows Dangerous

An important meeting occurred on March 21, 1973, between Nixon and White House aides John W. Dean III and H.R. Haldeman. Dean had been overseeing the attempt to cover-up Watergate, and he told Nixon the cover-up itself had become as potentially harmful to his presidency as the burglary. Dean said, "I think that there's no doubt about the seriousness of the problem we've got. We have a cancer within, close to the Presidency, that's growing. It's growing daily. It's compounding, it grows geometrically now, because it compounds itself."[62]

The cover-up was growing more dangerous because Nixon aides were bribing the burglars to remain silent about what really happened. Payments to the men, including Hunt and Liddy, involved in the burglary for trial costs and living expenses began soon after they were arrested, and between them they received more than four hundred thousand dollars in the first eight months after the break-in. Nixon himself knew about the payments from the beginning. On August 1, 1972, Haldeman told Nixon the burglars had been released from jail and had been "taken care of." When Nixon asked if that had cost a lot, Haldeman told him, "It's very expensive," to which the president replied, "Well, they have to be paid. That's all there is to that. They have to be paid."[63]

As the January 1973 trial approached, Nixon aides became even more worried that the burglars would reveal the truth. On January 6, two days before the trial began, Dean telephoned Liddy. He promised to pay the men involved in the burglary to be silent about their connection to the White House if they were convicted and sent to prison so they would have money for their families. Liddy said Dean told him "Gordon, I want to assure you, everyone's going to be taken care of—everyone."[64] Dean, for example, promised Liddy thirty thousand dollars a year and a pardon within two years for any crimes for which he was convicted.

The other men were also offered various sums of money. After the legal proceedings against them were over, they demanded more money for their silence. On March 21, Nixon and Haldeman discussed the need for more money for bribes. Nixon told Haldeman he was willing to spend another one million dollars to continue buying the silence of the seven men.

But the day before Nixon discussed the bribes with Haldeman, McCord gave his letter to Sirica saying he was willing to testify truthfully about what happened. And on March 28, McCord began revealing details about the connection between the burglars and the Nixon administra-tion. Nixon would have even more to worry about soon because one of his key aides had also decided to tell the truth.

Dean Tells the Truth

In his March 21 meeting with Nixon, Dean admitted he was worried that he and other White House aides could be charged in connection with the cover-up if it became public. When Dean learned soon afterward that McCord was going to testify, he became more frightened that he was in serious trouble for helping direct the cover-up, including bribing the burglars.

A few days after the March 21 meeting, Haldeman told Dean that the president

The accused Watergate burglars stand outside the district court with their attorney. They are, from left to right, Virgilio Gonzales, Frank Sturgis, attorney Henry Rothblatt, Bernard Barker, and Eugenio Martinez.

$1 Million for Bribes

One of the Watergate crimes that really bothered the American public was the Nixon administration's attempt to silence the men who committed the burglary by paying them bribes. President Richard M. Nixon knew about the illegal payments. In fact, in a White House conversation on March 21, 1973, Nixon told John W. Dean III he could get $1 million to continue paying the men so they would not cooperate with any investigation. Nixon also told Dean he could get that huge sum in cash, which probably would have involved illegal cash contributions from Nixon's campaign donors. The following exchange between Dean and the president took place after Dean told Nixon more money was needed for bribery:

PRESIDENT NIXON: How much money do you need?

DEAN: I would say these people are going to cost a million dollars over the next two years.

PRESIDENT NIXON: We could get that. If you need the money, you could get the money. What I mean is, you could, you could get a million dollars. And you could get it in cash. I, I know where it could be gotten. I mean it's not easy, but it could be done.

Quoted in Stanley I. Kutler, ed., *Abuse of Power: The New Nixon Tapes*. New York: Simon and Schuster, 1997, p. 254.

wanted him to write a report summarizing everything that had happened involving Watergate. But he asked Dean to lie in the report and say that neither the president nor his top aides knew about Watergate. Dean believed Nixon wanted him to write the report so that, if the truth was ever revealed, he could claim Dean masterminded the burglary and cover-up and then lied about it to protect himself. After thinking it over for several days, Dean decided not to write the report. Several years later Dean wrote,

"[My] thoughts finally headed down the path I knew I had to explore. The path of telling the truth. Whatever else happened in the days, weeks and months ahead, I was not going to lie for anybody, even the President. Despite what I'd done for him, I would not take that step."[65]

Dean began meeting with federal prosecutors in early April. In return for his cooperation, Dean wanted leniency for crimes he had committed. When Nixon learned Dean was cooperating with officials, he knew he was in serious trouble because Dean could testify he had personally been involved in the cover-up. Nixon decided he had to show the public that he was doing something to clean up the Watergate mess.

On the evening of April 30, Nixon went on television in his first major speech about Watergate. Nixon claimed he had known nothing about the burglary and possible cover-up until March, when he learned that some of the allegations concerning his staff might be true. The president said he then ordered a new investigation into the matter to find out what had happened. "I was determined that we should get to the bottom of the matter, and that the truth should be fully brought out no matter who was involved,"[66] Nixon told the nation.

The president then announced the resignations of presidential aides Dean, Haldeman, and John Ehrlichman and Attorney General Richard Kleindienst. A president appoints aides and cabinet members, like Kleindienst, and can force them to resign at any time. The president was trying to protect himself by denying he knew about Watergate and getting rid

John Dean testifying on the Watergate case before the Senate committee on June 27, 1973. Dean's testimony linked Nixon directly with the cover-up.

of people close to him who were involved in it. Kleindienst had not been involved in the cover-up but was forced to leave because he claimed the FBI, which was under his jurisdiction, was not doing a good job investigating Watergate.

Nixon never said any of the four had done anything wrong, and he even praised Haldeman and Erlichman as fine government officials. Most people, however, assumed that all four had resigned because they had done something wrong even if the president did not say so.

The "Toothpaste" Was Out

Nixon lied in his televised Watergate speech by saying he had not known anything about Watergate, because he had participated in covering up facts about it. The speech was simply an attempt to persuade the public that he had not done anything wrong. However, when Dean decided to talk to prosecutors, it was

Haldeman Resigns

On April 29, 1973, President Richard M. Nixon invited H.R. "Bob" Haldeman to Camp David, the presidential retreat in Maryland. Nixon told Haldeman he was going to ask him and John Ehrlichman to resign because of the Watergate scandal. In his book *The Ends of Power*, Haldeman writes that Nixon told him how anguished he was about having to make them quit:

> Nixon said with a hushed voice, "You know, Bob, there's something I've never told anybody before, not even you. Every night since I've been President, every single night before I've gone to bed, I've knelt down on my knees beside my bed and prayed to God for guidance and help in this job." I was deeply touched by this. He went on: "Last night before I went to bed I knelt down and this time I prayed I wouldn't wake up in the morning. I just couldn't face going on." "Mr. President," I said, "you can't indulge yourself in that kind of feeling. You've got to go on. If there are other problems, they have to be dealt with, that's all."

Haldeman also writes that he was touched that Nixon had shared his innermost thoughts with him. But when Haldeman later discovered that Nixon had told Ehrlichman the same thing, he admitted "This hurt me."

H.R. Haldeman with Joseph DiMona, *The Ends of Power*. New York: Times Books, 1978, p. 448.

inevitable that Nixon's role in Watergate would be exposed.

When Haldeman learned that Dean was meeting with prosecutors, he told Dean to be careful about what he said because "once the toothpaste is out of the tube it's going to be very hard to get it back in."[67] In the next few months, the testimony of Dean and other Nixon aides would release all the "toothpaste," which was the truth about Watergate.

Chapter Five

Hearings, Tapes, and Impeachment

President Richard M. Nixon installed a system in the Oval Office to record telephone calls and conversations to create an historical record of his presidency. Nixon regretted that decision after the Watergate burglary, because he realized the tapes could incriminate him and his aides in the incident and other illegal activities. On June 20, 1972, just three days after the Watergate break-in, Nixon discussed the threat the tapes posed to him with H.R. Haldeman:

PRESIDENT NIXON: This oval office business [i.e. the taping system] complicates things all over.

HALDEMAN: They say it's extremely good. I haven't listened to the tapes.

PRESIDENT NIXON: They're kept for future purposes.[68]

This exchange is from the first-known taped conversation in which Nixon discusses Watergate. Nixon and Haldeman talked about how the burglary would affect Nixon's chance for reelection, especially if James W. McCord Jr. and E. Howard Hunt could be linked to the White House. The talk proves Nixon knew his aides were involved in Watergate shortly after it happened. In 1972, however, only a few people in the Nixon administration knew that the taping system itself existed. The public would not learn about the incriminating tapes for another year, and then only through the efforts of several high-level government investigations that were trying to discover the truth about Watergate.

Senate and Justice Department Investigations

On February 7, 1973, the Senate voted 77–0 to create a Select Committee on Presidential Campaign Activities to investigate political crimes that occurred during the 1972 campaign. It became known as the Watergate committee because its probe focused on that incident. Four Democrats, Sam J. Ervin of North Carolina, Daniel K. Inouye of Hawaii, Joseph M. Montoya of New Mexico, and Herman E. Talmadge of Georgia, and three Republicans, Howard H. Baker Jr. of Tennessee, Edward J. Gurney of Florida, and Lowell P. Weicker Jr. of Connecticut were the members of the committee.

When Ervin was chosen to chair the committee, Nixon said, "Thank god it's Ervin."[69] Nixon believed Ervin was too old, at the age of seventy-six, and not skillful enough to direct an investigation that could discover the truth. But Ervin's folksy mannerisms and speech belied the intelligence and ability that had made him a successful senator for two decades. When the committee held its first Watergate hearing on May 17, 1973, Ervin's dramatic opening statement showed he was much more able than Nixon believed. Ervin said,

If the many allegations made to this date are true, then the burglars who broke into the headquarters of the Democratic National Committee at the Watergate were in effect breaking

Nixon meets with his chief of staff H.R. Haldeman in the Oval Office in 1971. Recordings of their conversations about Watergate ultimately exposed Nixon's involvement with the scandal.

Sam Ervin, speaking at center, sits among members of the Senate Watergate Investigating committee in 1973. Nixon wrongly believed Ervin would not be skillful enough to direct the investigation.

into the home of every citizen of the United States. And if these allegations prove to be true, what they were seeking to steal was not the jewels, money or other precious property of American citizens, but something much more valuable—their most precious heritage: the right to vote in a free election.[70]

Ervin's eloquent statement made Americans realize the burglary was not just another political trick one party had played on another but an attempt to deny Americans their right to freely choose their president. The power of Ervin's words was magnified by the fact

that the hearing was broadcast live on national television.

The day after that first hearing, attorney general–designate Elliot L. Richardson launched a separate investigation into the Watergate incident. Richardson named former government attorney Archibald Cox as the Justice Department's special Watergate prosecutor. Nixon named Richardson attorney general after Richard Kleindienst resigned on April 30. Cox said his investigation was important because it could restore the public's faith in its ability to elect public officials. "Somehow," Cox said, "we must restore confidence, honor and integrity in government."[71] As a special prosecutor,

Impeaching a President

The U.S. Constitution gives Congress the power to remove a president from office through a process called impeachment. The Constitution authorizes the U.S. House of Representatives to impeach the president by charging the president with specific charges, each of which is called an "article of impeachment." If the House votes to impeach a president, the Constitution then gives the Senate the power to try the president on the articles of impeachment. At least two-thirds of senators must vote for conviction on the articles of impeachment to remove the president from office. President Richard M. Nixon resigned on August 8, 1974, before the House could impeach him. The House has impeached two presidents—Andrew Johnson in 1868 and Bill Clinton in 1998—but the Senate failed to convict either of them. Johnson was impeached by congressmen who believed his plans for dealing with Southern states after the Civil War were too lenient. Clinton was impeached for allegedly lying about a sexual affair with a White House intern and for trying to obstruct an investigation into the affair. Johnson and Clinton were both Democrats and were impeached by Republican-controlled Houses. Historians believe the impeachments came about mainly due to political rivalry between the two parties.

Cox would have more freedom to investigate the Watergate burglary than someone who worked for the Justice Department, which was controlled by the president.

Cox and the Senate were investigating Watergate even after the burglars had been convicted, because there were still so many unanswered questions. These official probes elevated Watergate from a minor burglary to a headline-making news event.

The Watergate Hearings

The Watergate hearings were some of the most sensational and widely watched programs ever televised. During the next few months, 319 hours of hearings were shown and an estimated 85 percent of all U.S. households watched at least part of them. The hearings were also broadcast on radio stations. Millions of people turned on the hearings instead of their favorite soap operas and game shows because they felt they were watching history being made. There was also a morbid fascination for viewers in seeing witnesses squirm while answering tough questions. On the first day of the hearings, Ronald Coleman, a graduate of Catholic University in Washington, D.C., summed up why it was fun to watch: "We've all got a little sadistic streak in us—like stopping on the highway to watch an accident."[72]

People watch the Watergate hearings in the television section of a department store in 1973. The hearings became some of the most widely watched television programs ever.

Although the hearings focused on Watergate, details emerged about other illegal White House activities. On June 13, the committee released a memorandum addressed to former Nixon aide John Ehrlichman that described the plan to burglarize the office of Daniel Ellsberg's psychiatrist. The news of White House involvement in the crime shook people's confidence in Nixon and made more people believe he could have participated in Watergate.

The star witness of the hearings was John Dean III. In testimony that began on May 25, Dean explained how he and other presidential aides covered up Watergate. Some of Dean's most damaging testimony came when he described a meeting he had with Nixon on September 15, 1972. Dean testified that after the talk, he believed Nixon knew about the attempted cover-up. Dean said, "I left with the impression that the President was well aware of what had been going on regarding the success of keeping the White House out of the Watergate scandal, and I also had expressed to him my concern that I was not confident the cover-up could be maintained indefinitely."[73]

Americans were stunned to learn Nixon knew about the cover-up but did not stop it. Dean's statement raised many questions about what Nixon knew about Watergate. Committee member Baker summed up what senators wanted to find out when he asked Dean, "What did the president know and when did he know it?"[74] That information was key because it would prove Nixon knew about the burglary and participated in the cover-up.

The Watergate committee and Cox knew it would be hard to discover those answers. But they soon found the key to finding them from former presidential aide Alexander Butterfield. On July 13, the committee members asked Butterfield if there were any recording devices in Nixon's office. Butterfield responded, "I was hoping you fellows wouldn't ask me that."[75] He then explained that Nixon had been taping telephone calls and meetings in the Oval Office.

Senate staff members had not known about the system and had only been asking random questions to see if Butterfield

knew anything that would be valuable to the investigation. But Cox and the committee realized immediately that the tapes were a key source of information about Nixon's role in Watergate. On July 23 Cox asked Nixon for tapes from certain days; he based his requests on testimony from Dean and other witnesses on when they had spoken with Nixon about Watergate.

Their demands touched off a bitter fight for control of the tapes, one that would ultimately decide Nixon's future.

The President Fights Back

When Nixon learned that investigators knew about the tapes, he became so frightened that he ordered the White

Shown here is the original letter Nixon wrote to Judge Sirica claiming he did not have to honor the subpoena and turn over the tapes because he was president.

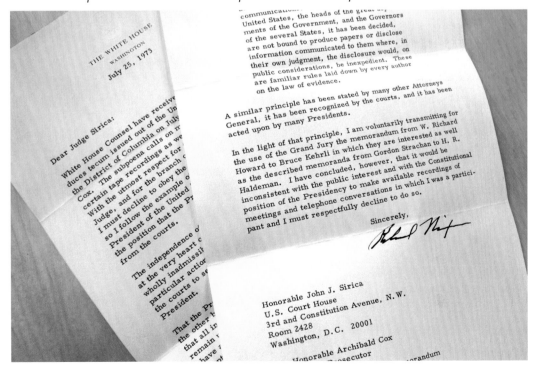

House taping system disconnected. Because Nixon realized how much damaging information was on the tapes, he decided to fight to keep the tapes secret. Nixon refused to give the tapes to investigators, but Cox and Ervin persuaded federal judge John Sirica to issue a subpoena, a written court order that would force Nixon to release them or face obstruction of justice charges. On July 26 Nixon again refused to surrender the tapes. In a letter to Sirica, Nixon claimed he did not have to honor the subpoena because he was the president. Nixon wrote, "The independence of the three branches of our government is at the very heart of our Constitutional system. It would be [wrong] for the President to seek to compel some particular action by the courts. It is equally [wrong] for the courts to seek to compel some particular action from the President."[76]

Nixon based his refusal on executive privilege, a legal theory that claims the Constitution guarantees presidents should be free of control by the courts or Congress in carrying out their essential duties. Cox and Ervin appealed Nixon's refusal and it would take several months for the federal court system to decide the legal issues involved.

The Watergate committee meanwhile had recessed its hearings in early August. Nixon used the break to claim he had not done anything wrong. "Not only was I unaware of any cover-up but I was unaware of anything to cover up,"[77] Nixon said in an August 15 television speech.

Most people, however, no longer believed Nixon. In addition to continuing revelations about his involvement in Watergate, federal investigators were also uncovering evidence that Nixon's 1972 presidential campaign had accepted millions of dollars in illegal contributions. The allegations further tainted Nixon's reputation as did his continuing fight to withhold the tapes; many people believed he was fighting the court order to conceal his guilt.

On October 12, a federal appeals court upheld Cox's right to the tapes. Nixon then made another attempt to conceal incriminating evidence. Nixon offered to have Republican senator John C. Stennis, a political ally, review and summarize the conversations instead of releasing them. When Cox refused that compromise, Nixon decided to fire him to keep the tapes from being made public.

"I'm Not a Crook"

On Saturday, October 20 Nixon's chief of staff, Alexander Haig, at Nixon's request, ordered Attorney General Elliot Richardson to fire Archibald Cox. Richardson refused because he believed it was wrong for a president to use his power to interfere in a criminal investigation involving himself. "A government of the laws was on the verge of becoming a government of one man,"[78] Richardson said. Richardson resigned rather than fire Cox. Haig then asked Deputy Attorney General William Ruckelshaus to fire Cox. When Ruckelshaus also refused, Nixon fired him. Haig finally persuaded Solicitor General Robert Bork to fire Cox.

Expletive Deleted

Richard M. Nixon wanted his conversations and telephone calls taped to provide an accurate record of his presidency. To his later dismay, they helped prove his involvement in Watergate. The National Archives and Records Administration has released more than two thousand hours of Nixon tapes. The conversations provide an intimate and not always pleasant portrait of the former president. Nixon used so many swear words in his private talks that newspapers and magazines had to leave them out when they printed them. To show readers where the obscenities had been edited out, newspapers inserted the phrase "expletive deleted" in parentheses. Historian Stanley I. Kutler said the vile language shocked many people, including Nixon's political supporters. In his book, *Abuse of Power*, Kutler writes,

> Before [the tapes'] release, the President had labored desperately to delete references to Jesus Christ [and other profanities]. Nonetheless, the President's congressional allies, his friends, and friendly columnists were appalled. Senate Minority leader Hugh School called [the profanities] "shabby, disgusting, and immoral"; even Vice President Gerald Ford found [Nixon's foul language] "a little disappointing." William Safire, a longtime Nixon aide and by then a *New York Times* columnist, thought the conversations revealed a man "guilty of conduct unbecoming a President." The Rev. Billy Graham, a faithful supporter, could not "but deplore the moral tone implied."

Stanley I. Kutler, ed., *Abuse of Power: The New Nixon Tapes*. New York: Simon and Schuster, 1997, p. xv.

The president also abolished the office of special prosecutor and turned the investigation over to the Justice Department so that he could better control it.

Nixon's maneuver to evade criminal prosecution backfired. The news media nicknamed the series of events the Saturday Night Massacre. Newspaper and magazine editorials condemned Nixon for his actions, with many of them calling for his resignation, and news reports created a wave of public outrage against the president. The growing Nixon backlash forced him to reverse what he had done. Nixon reinstated the Special Prosecutor's Office and on November 1 named Leon Jaworski to replace Cox. The president also agreed to give transcripts of some of the subpoenaed tapes to Watergate investigators.

But when investigators received the transcripts on November 15, they discovered that a tape of conversations from June 23, 1972, had an unexplained eighteen-and-a-half minute gap. The missing audio was important because Haldeman had testified that he and Nixon discussed Watergate that day. The White House claimed Rose Mary Woods, Nixon's secretary, had accidentally erased the segment while transcribing the tape. Investigators and the public, however, believed the tape had been erased on purpose to protect Nixon.

On November 17, Nixon defended himself in a speech to newspaper editors in Orlando, Florida. Nixon's defense was summed up by two sentences: "People have got to know whether or not their President is a crook. Well, I'm not a crook."[79] Many people, even those who did not believe Nixon was guilty of anything, thought it was sad that a president had to declare he was not a criminal.

The Battle for the Tapes Continues

Nixon realized he had made a mistake in releasing the tapes. In December Nixon declared he would not surrender any more tapes and on January 24, 1974, he refused a request from the Senate

Members of the U.S. House of Representatives listen to the Watergate tapes on August 6, 1974.

committee for documents concerning Watergate. Nixon again claimed executive privilege, telling the senators that "to produce the material you now seek would unquestionably destroy any vestige of confidentiality of Presidential communications, thereby irreparably impairing the constitutional functions of the Office of the Presidency."[80]

The fight for the tapes was renewed on April 11 when Jaworski and the House Judiciary Committee requested more tapes. The judiciary committee had begun investigating Watergate in December to see if there was enough evidence to impeach Nixon. Impeachment is the power the U.S. Constitution grants Congress to remove presidents who have committed crimes. Because of its power to impeach Nixon, the judiciary committee's investigation now became more important than that of the Senate Watergate committee. The Senate committee, which was nearly finished with its investigation, gave its evidence to the House Judiciary Committee and cooperated with its probe of the president.

Nixon at first refused to surrender the tapes because they showed he had been involved in the cover-up. One especially damning conversation occurred on March 21, 1973, when Nixon and Dean discussed bribing the convicted burglars. But on April 29, 1974, Nixon released twelve hundred pages of heavily edited transcripts of the tapes. Nixon had to release the transcripts to avoid being charged with contempt of Congress, an offense that warranted impeachment. On March 22, 1974, a depressed Nixon wrote in his diary, "Lowest day. Contempt equals impeachment."[81]

Jaworski and the committee rejected the transcripts and demanded the tapes. When Judge Sirica ruled that Nixon had to release them, Nixon appealed the order to the U.S. Supreme Court. Nixon's action again created a public furor and increased demands by elected officials, the news media, and citizens that he resign or be impeached.

On July 24, 1974, the Supreme Court, in a unanimous 8–0 decision, upheld the right of investigators to hear the tapes (the court has nine members but Justice William Rehnquist declined to vote because he had been appointed by Nixon). The ruling, read by Chief Justice Warren Burger, said a president could not use executive privilege to withhold evidence in criminal proceedings. Nixon had to release tapes, which included recordings of conversations that proved he had known about and helped direct the cover-up of Watergate.

Impeaching the President

Three days later the judiciary committee began formal televised hearings on whether to impeach the president of the United States. The first hearing opened with statements from committee members on why the hearings were important. No one was more impressive than Representative Barbara Jordan, a Texas Democrat. According to Jordan, the Constitution demands that Congress remove any president who has committed illegal acts. She said,

Has the President committed offenses, and planned, and directed,

A demonstration is held outside the White House supporting the impeachment of President Nixon following the Watergate scandal.

and acquiesced in a course of conduct which the Constitution will not tolerate? That's the question. We know that. We know the question. We should now forthwith proceed to answer the question. It is reason, and not passion, which must guide our deliberations, guide our debate, and guide our decision.[82]

For several months before the hearings started, judiciary committee members had considered documents, tapes, and testimony gathered by the Senate Watergate committee, special prosecutors, and its own staff. So it did not take the committee long to decide on whether Nixon should be impeached. On July 27 the committee voted 27–11 to approve the first article of impeachment, which charged Nixon with obstruction of justice for using his office to try to stop or hamper Watergate investigations. In the next few days, the committee approved two other articles of impeachment against Nixon: abuse of his power for political purposes by violating the rights of citizens with wiretaps and burglaries and contempt of Congress for refusing to honor its subpoenas for evidence.

Six Republicans joined the Democratic majority in voting to impeach Nixon. Republican representative Caldwell Butler of Virginia explains why he voted to impeach Nixon: "The pattern of misrepresentation and half-truth that emerges from our investigation reveals a presidential policy cynically based on the premise that truth itself is negotiable."[83]

The committee recommended to the House of Representatives that Nixon be impeached on all three charges. The House then scheduled an impeachment vote for August 19. If the House, as expected, voted to impeach Nixon, the U.S. Senate would try him on the charges. If Nixon was found guilty, he would be removed from office.

Resign or Be Impeached?

Many members of Congress had said they would not vote to impeach Nixon unless there was a "smoking gun,"— undeniable proof that he had been involved in Watergate. But when the White House finally released the tapes on August 5, 1974, Nixon realized that his June 23, 1972, conversation with Haldeman that was still on the tape was the smoking gun that would likely mean his impeachment. After the July 24 Supreme Court decision, Nixon realized that the full story of his involvement in the cover-up would be made public if he was impeached. Nixon began to consider resigning in order to avoid the embarrassment of going through such a humiliating procedure. However, he delayed a final decision on resigning

Nixon's Resignation Speech

In his televised speech the night of August 8, 1974, President Richard M. Nixon told Americans he was resigning because it was the best thing for the nation. Nixon said,

Throughout the long and difficult period of Watergate, I have felt it was my duty to persevere, to make every possible effort to complete the term of office to which you elected me. In the past few days, however, it has become evident to me that I no longer have a strong enough political base [to] justify continuing that effort. As long as there was such a base, I felt strongly that it was necessary to see the constitutional process through to its conclusion. [But] with the disappearance of that base, I now believe that the constitutional purpose has been served, and there is no longer a need for the process to be prolonged. I would have preferred to carry through to the finish whatever the personal agony it would have involved, and my family unanimously urged me to do so. But the interest of the Nation must always come before any personal considerations. [I] have never been a quitter. To leave office before my term is completed is abhorrent to every instinct in my body. But as President, I must put the interest of America first.

Richard M. Nixon, resignation speech, August 8, 1974, Public Broadcasting System, www.pbs.org/ newshour/character/links/nixon_speech.html.

until he learned what Congress would do to him.

On August 7 Nixon met with three Republican congressional leaders—Senators Barry Goldwater of Arizona and Hugh Scott of Pennsylvania and Representative John Rhodes of Arizona. "Mr. President," Goldwater said, "this isn't pleasant, but you want to know the situation and it isn't good."[84] Rhodes told Nixon the House would vote to impeach him and Goldwater and Scott said they and other senators would vote to find him guilty in the Senate impeachment trial.

The news made Nixon realize he had to resign before he was impeached. He met later with Haig and press secretary Ron Ziegler to tell them his decision. Nixon said "Well, I screwed it up real good, didn't I?"[85] The weak joke concealed Nixon's feelings of despair and sadness at having to resign. Nixon told Ziegler to schedule a televised speech for the next evening so he could announce his resignation to the nation. On August 8, 1974, Nixon met during the day with cabinet members and other staff members to tell them he was resigning. One of his most important meetings was with Vice President Gerald Ford, who under the Constitution would become president when Nixon resigned. "Jerry, I know you'll do a good job,"[86] Nixon told him.

At 9 P.M. that night, Nixon told a television audience of 150 million people that he was resigning. Nixon mentioned Watergate but did not admit any guilt. Nixon claimed he was stepping down because his loss of support in Congress and among U.S. citizens had weakened his ability to effectively govern the nation. Nixon did admit that his presidency had created great political divisions. Nixon said, "By taking this action I hope that I will have hastened the start of the process of healing which is so desperately needed in America."[87]

Nixon announced that his resignation would be effective at noon on August 9. On that day, he would become the first president to resign from the world's most powerful government position.

Chapter Six

The Aftermath

Richard M. Nixon woke up about 6 A.M. on August 9, 1974, the 2,027th and final day of his presidency. After eating breakfast, Nixon began writing a farewell speech to members of his cabinet and White House staff. Alexander Haig, his chief of staff, interrupted Nixon while he was working. "This is something that will have to be done, Mr. President, and I thought you would rather do it now," Haig said. He handed Nixon a paper with a single line of type that read "I hereby resign the Office of President of the United States."[88] Nixon signed the resignation and returned to his speech.

At 9:30 A.M., Nixon entered the East Room of the White House to "Hail to the Chief," the tune reserved for the president that was being played for the last time in his honor. Nixon was accompanied by his wife, Pat, and daughters, Julie and Tricia, and their husbands. Nixon fought back tears while delivering his farewell in a choked voice. Many in the audience wept openly as he addressed them.

Nixon rarely showed the sentimental side of his personality. But he talked about how much his parents had meant to him and what an honor it had been to live in the White House. Nixon admitted that "we have done some things wrong in this Administration," but did not say what those errors were. In what was the saddest and most humiliating moment of his life, Nixon tried to sound upbeat as he said,

Always give your best, never get discouraged, never be petty; always remember, others may hate you, but those who hate you don't win unless you hate them, and then you destroy yourself. And so, we leave with high hopes, in good spirit, and with deep humility, and with very much gratefulness in our hearts.[89]

Nixon and his family then went outside to climb into a waiting U.S. Army helicopter. Nixon spoke briefly to Vice President Gerald R. Ford and then began climbing the stairs into the aircraft. At the top of the stairway, Nixon turned and gave one final wave to staff members. Nixon then raised both arms and extended his fingers in his trademark double-V victory salute before finally entering the aircraft.

The helicopter lifted off at 10:01 A.M. and transported the Nixons to Andrews Air Force Base in Maryland, where they boarded a plane for San Clemente, California. Nixon's letter of resignation was given to Secretary of State Henry Kissinger at 11:35 A.M., ending one of the most turbulent presidencies in U.S. history. Nixon's resignation, however, did not end the legal and political storms over Watergate.

Indict Nixon or Not?

At 12:03 P.M. on August 9, 1974, Gerald R. Ford took the oath of office as president in the White House East Room. Technically, he had been president since 11:35 A.M. when Nixon's resignation was delivered to the secretary of state. Ford became the thirty-eighth president and was the first to take office under the 25th Amendment, which empowers the vice president to succeed the president if he dies, resigns, or is removed from office. He was also the first president who had not been elected either president or vice president.

Nixon gives his farewell speech to his staff, while his daughter Tricia and son-in-law Edward look on.

Gerald Ford (right) takes the oath of office following the resignation of Richard Nixon.

Ford said, "I assume the Presidency under extraordinary circumstances never before experienced by Americans. This is an hour of history that troubles our minds and hurts our hearts."[90] Although he did not refer directly to Watergate or Nixon's departure in disgrace, Ford claimed, "My fellow Americans, our long national nightmare is over."[91]

But the anguish Americans had experienced over Watergate for two years was not over because officials were still trying participants for crimes they had committed. In fact, Americans were still wondering if the former president would be prosecuted even though he had resigned. The likelihood that Nixon could face some sort of prosecution seemed to increase on August 20 when the House of Representatives voted 412–3 to accept the House Judiciary Committee report recommending his impeachment. Although Nixon's resignation had made impeachment unnecessary, the vote showed how many members of Congress believed he was guilty of Watergate crimes.

It was now up to special Watergate prosecutor Leon Jaworski to determine if Nixon should be brought to trial. Jaworski solicited recommendations on

Nixon's "True Crime"

According to historian Theodore H. White, who has written widely about U.S. presidents and how they are elected, Richard M. Nixon's real crime was to tarnish the office of the president. In his book, *Breach of Faith*, White writes

> The true crime of Richard Nixon was simple: he destroyed the myth that binds America together, and for this he was driven from power. The myth he broke was critical—that somewhere in American life there is at least one man who stands for law, the President. That faith surmounts all daily cynicism, all evidence of suspicion of wrongdoing by lesser leaders, all corruptions, all vulgarities, all the ugly compromises of daily striving and ambition. That faith holds that all men are equal before the law and protected by it; and that no matter how the faith may be betrayed elsewhere, at one particular point—the Presidency—justice will be done beyond prejudice, beyond rancor, beyond the possibility of a fix. It was that faith that Richard Nixon broke, betraying those who voted for him even more than those who voted against him.

Theodore H. White, *Breach of Faith: The Fall of Richard Nixon*. New York: Atheneum, 1975, p. 322.

what to do from staff members who had investigated Watergate. In a memorandum to Jaworski, attorney George Frampton wrote, "I fear that history may yet judge this venture [the investigation] a failure should your decision be to 'call it a day' and not indict former President Nixon."[92] But, Frampton noted, public sentiment was that Nixon had suffered enough by having to resign. He also questioned whether Nixon could get a fair trial. Many people believed a fair trial was impossible because prospective jurors, having been exposed to news media coverage about Watergate, had probably already made up their minds about his guilt or innocence.

Nixon was worried that Jaworski's decision could be influenced by demands from the news media that he be charged. "They won't be satisfied until they have me in jail,"[93] Nixon told his former aides. However, Nixon's fate was soon taken out of Jaworski's hands by President Ford.

The Pardon

When Nixon resigned, many people believed he had struck a deal with Ford. Nixon would resign so Ford could become president, and Ford would pardon Nixon so he would not have to stand trial for any Watergate crimes. The theory seemed believable, because the public had learned about a meeting on August 1 between Haig and Ford. Haig met with the vice president to alert him that Nixon was considering resigning, and Ford had to prepare to assume the presidency. In that meeting Haig also gave Ford a list of options on how to handle Watergate when he became president, one of which was to pardon Nixon.

Haig and Ford both later denied that they had made a deal to pardon Nixon. However, Ford must have at least been considering a pardon from the time he became president. When Ford was asked on August 28 at his first press conference as president about a possible pardon, he replied, "It is an option and a proper option for any president."[94] And only eleven days later on September 8, Ford announced that he was pardoning the former president.

In a televised speech, Ford told Americans that he felt sympathy for Nixon for the disgrace and humiliation he and his family had already suffered. But Ford said he was not pardoning Nixon because he felt sorry for him. Ford believed that legal proceedings against Nixon would further inflame the divisiveness and bitterness Watergate had created. He said, "[My] conscience tells me clearly and certainly that I cannot prolong the bad dreams that continue to reopen a chapter that is closed. My conscience tells me that only I, as President, have the constitutional power to firmly shut and seal this book. My concern is the immediate future of this great country."[95]

The pardon covered any crimes Nixon committed as president. In accepting the pardon—an act many people believed proved he was guilty of the crimes that the House had charged him with—Nixon said, "No words can describe the depths of my regret and pain at the anguish which my mistakes over Watergate have caused the nation and the presidency."[96] Nixon admitted to having made "mistakes," but many people were disappointed he did not admit he had done something illegal or morally wrong.

A Gallup poll showed 53 percent of Americans opposed the pardon, because they wanted Nixon to stand trial. Many people also thought it was unfair for Nixon to be pardoned while many other people were still being tried and sentenced for Watergate crimes.

Nixon Wrecked Their Lives

On March 1, 1974, the grand jury that had been considering Watergate charges since the burglary occurred indicted former U.S. attorney general John N. Mitchell and six White House aides—H.R. Haldeman, John Ehrlichman, Charles Colson, Gordon C. Strachan, Robert Mardian, and Kenneth Parkinson—for obstructing the investigation. The grand jury named Nixon as a coconspirator but did not charge him with any crimes. The "Watergate Seven" were tried by federal judge John Sirica. On January 1, 1975, all but Parkinson were found guilty of various charges of trying to obstruct the Watergate investigation and conceal Nixon's participation in the cover-up. Mardian was later cleared of all charges in a second trial.

When Mitchell was found guilty of conspiracy, obstruction of justice, and perjury charges, he became the first former U.S. attorney general convicted of illegal activities and imprisoned. Sirica sentenced Mitchell to up to eight years in prison; he only served nineteen months before being released because of poor health. Mitchell had only himself to blame, because he had approved G. Gordon Liddy's plan to bug the Democratic National Committee offices. Yet Mitchell once angrily declared that when they met "I should have thrown Liddy out the window."[97]

Sirica was also the judge who tried and sentenced Liddy and the other men involved in the burglary—E. Howard Hunt, Bernard L. Barker, Virgilio R. Gonzalez, Eugenio R. Martinez, Frank A. Sturgis, and James W. McCord Jr. Before Sirica sentenced them on March 23, 1973, he said, "The crimes committed by these defendants can only be described as sordid, despicable, and thoroughly reprehensible."[98] Liddy received the stiffest sentence and served fifty-two months in prison. The others had shorter sentences, because their crimes were less serious or they cooperated with authorities. McCord, whose testimony helped investigators discover the truth about Watergate, was in prison only four months.

Other top aides like John Dean III and Jeb Magruder were among thirty

Watergate mastermind G. Gordon Liddy received the stiffest sentence for his role in the scandal, serving just over four years in prison.

The President's Aides

Many people believe it was unfair that President Nixon escaped punishment for his involvement in Watergate even though many of his aides were tried, convicted, and sent to prison. White House aides H.R. Haldeman, John Ehrlichman, Charles Colson, and John W. Dean III all went to prison along with other Watergate figures like G. Gordon Liddy, who helped plan and carry out the burglary of the Democratic National Committee offices. But many of the central figures in Watergate benefited from the notoriety they gained from the political scandal after they were released from prison. Dean received $1 million for writing a book about his experiences. He was just one of many Watergate figures from Haldeman and Liddy to Judge John J. Sirica who were paid well to author books about their part in the historic event. Liddy served the longest sentence, nearly five years. When Liddy got out of prison, he capitalized on his Watergate fame and became a radio talk-show host and played small parts in movies and on television shows. Haldeman sold real estate and opened steak houses. He once said that instead of hurting him, his Watergate fame helped him in his business deals.

individuals who pled guilty and were indicted or convicted of charges related to Watergate or other illegal 1972 campaign activities, such as burglarizing the office of Daniel Ellsberg's psychiatrist. Twenty-one corporations including American Airlines, Goodyear, and Hertz were also found guilty of giving illegal contributions to Nixon's campaign. Another casualty of Watergate was President Ford. Democrat Jimmy Carter defeated Ford in the 1976 presidential election, and it was believed that lingering public anger over Nixon's pardon was responsible for Ford's loss.

Kissinger once summed up the scope of the Watergate damage saying, "In destroying himself, Nixon had wrecked the lives of almost all who had come into contact with him."[99] The irony of Watergate is that Nixon, the central figure in the worst political scandal in U.S. history, escaped untouched except for the humiliation of his resignation.

Nixon Bounces Back

While many of Nixon's former aides were imprisoned, Nixon was living at his luxurious oceanfront estate in San Clemente, California. Because of his involvement in Watergate, the state of New York took away his law license and he never practiced law again. Unable to work as a lawyer, Nixon began writing books and giving speeches. Nixon's infamy from Watergate helped him get a

Richard Nixon agreed to discuss his life and presidency with British newscaster David Frost, right, in 1977.

$2.5 million advance for writing his memoirs, which sold 330,000 copies in the first six months it was on sale in 1978.

Nixon was so desperate for money that in 1977 he agreed to a series of interviews with English television host David Frost. Nixon was paid six hundred thousand dollars plus a share of the profits from the sale of the interviews to television stations around the world. Frost recalled years later that "[Nixon] was obsessed with money."[100] Frost said Nixon feared that he would become poor if people who went to jail because of Watergate sued him. That never happened but it seemed a real threat at the time to Nixon.

Frost interviewed Nixon for nearly thirty hours, and the most fascinating questions and answers concerned Watergate. The interviews were developed into four television episodes, each ninety minutes long. When they were broadcast in the United States, the first episode drew an audience of 45 million viewers as people tuned in to see if Nixon would admit he had done something illegal. Nixon did not directly say he was guilty of any crimes. However, Nixon came close to confessing to his wrongdoing when he admitted, "I did abuse the power I had as president" and "I said things that were not true."[101] When Frost asked him if he had personally tried to conceal Watergate, Nixon replied, "Under the circumstances, I would have to say that a reasonable person would call [it] a cover-up. I let the American people down, and I have to carry that burden with me for the rest of my life. My political life is over."[102]

In the last nineteen years of his life, Nixon did everything he could to rehabilitate his public image. In his memoirs Nixon tried to downplay the importance of the burglary by comparing it to similar acts of political espionage that Democrats had committed. His greatest achievements were in foreign policy, and Nixon visited many foreign countries to remind people of what he had done. He also wrote several books about foreign affairs, which showed his understanding of such issues and garnered praise, even from people who disliked him for Watergate.

By the time Nixon died on April 22, 1994, he had acquired the status of elder statesman, who advised presidents and other officials about foreign affairs. Many people, however, never forgave him for Watergate and the ugly political division it created in the nation. At Nixon's funeral, Kissinger quoted a line from a play by Shakespeare to sum up the division of opinion that existed about Nixon. Kissinger said, "He was a man, take him

Scandalgate

The Watergate scandal has achieved a strange immortality by lending part of its name to other major political scandals. Journalists routinely attach the suffix "-gate" to disgraceful or criminal situations involving politicians or the government. Some examples are:

"Monicagate" was the sexual relationship President Bill Clinton had with White House intern Monica Lewinsky. When Clinton lied about the affair, the House of Representatives on December 19, 1998, impeached him on charges of perjury, obstruction of justice, and abuse of power. The Senate acquitted him on all charges in February 1999. Many felt the impeachment was a politically motivated Republican attempt to oust a Democratic president. Others felt that Congress had a duty to question the honesty and integrity of the president.

"Irangate" was a scandal in the 1980s that involved illegal activities by members of the administration of President Ronald Reagan, who sold weapons to Iran and diverted the proceeds to anti-Communist Contra rebels in Nicaragua.

"Katrinagate" was the federal government's failure in 2005 to adequately help victims of Hurricane Katrina.

for all in all. I shall not look upon his like again."[103] Kissinger used this famous quotation to remind people that before they judged Nixon, they should consider everything Nixon had done in his life, the good things as well as the bad things.

But when Nixon died, many people still believed his lasting legacy would be his disgraceful connection to Watergate. Today most people believe the political scandal itself has left a positive legacy.

The Legacy of Watergate

As chairman of the Senate Watergate committee, Senator Sam Ervin helped uncover the truth behind the burglary at the Watergate Hotel. On July 24, 1973, when Nixon refused for the first time to turn over White House tapes, Ervin was saddened about the political scandal that was growing larger every day. He said, "I think that the Watergate tragedy is the greatest tragedy this country has ever suffered."[104] Yet by 1982 Ervin had realized that there was a positive side to the nation's gravest political scandal. Ervin said the ability of Congress and the courts to control a president who was abusing the power of his office showed the strength of the nation's democratic system of government. He said, "It proves to me that we have the most viable government on the face of the earth. I don't think that kind of thing could happen in any country but ours … and that's all the more reason why we should keep this country great."[105]

The triumph of government that Ervin saw in Watergate was that the nation was able to survive an attempt by its most powerful official to cover up a crime without having the country fall into civil war. He believed that civil war could happen in a nation where the system of government does not have effective counterbalances to the power of the nation's leader. In 2007 Bob Woodward of the *Washington Post* also claimed Watergate had been beneficial for the United States. He said,

> Watergate was probably a good thing for the country; it was a good, sobering lesson. Accountability to the law applies to everyone. The problem with kings, and prime ministers, and presidents, is that they think they are above it, and there is no accountability, and that they have some special rights, and privileges, and statuses.[106]

In 1973 the *Washington Post* won the Pulitzer Prize for Public Service for Woodward and Carl Bernstein's reporting on Watergate. Their heroic work in helping to uncover the facts in Watergate inspired a generation of journalists to investigate such situations harder than ever before. In 1997 on the twenty-fifth anniversary of Watergate, historian Stephen Wayne of Georgetown University said the news media was still being affected positively by the political scandal. In the past reporters had sometimes failed to question the veracity of presidential statements because the office of president was so important. Wayne says that after Watergate, "the press no longer gives public officials the benefit of the doubt. [Reporters often] assume if a person is not lying, he's not telling the whole truth."[107] Wayne considers that attitude positive because it requires political figures to be more truthful with reporters, who serve as watchdogs for the public on any wrongdoing in government.

However, it is not only reporters who wound up having less respect and trust in presidents because of Watergate. According to Haig, Nixon tarnished the image of the presidency forever. He said, "Nixon will always be remembered for it because the event had such major historic consequences for the country; a fundamental discrediting of respect for the presidency—the integrity of the office."[108]

"Isn't It a Shame"

On April 30, 1973, after Nixon delivered his speech announcing the resignations of Haldeman and Ehrlichman, the president received a telephone call from Hobart D. Lewis, a supporter who was editor in chief of *Reader's Digest* magazine. After Lewis complimented Nixon on his speech, the president explained that it had been hard for him to fire two men who had been loyal to him for years. "Isn't it a shame," Nixon said, "it's all about a crappy little thing that didn't work? Didn't work. Nobody ever got a [expletive] thing out of the damn bugging."[109]

Nixon still believed Watergate was what Press Secretary Ron Ziegler had labeled a "third rate burglary."[110] According to historians, however the Watergate burglary was important, because it brought down a U.S. president and made more people aware that even presidents can do bad things.

Notes

Introduction: The Political Scandal That Ousted a President

1. Bill Clinton, "Eulogy for Former President Richard M. Nixon," *Vital Speeches of the Day.* June 1994, p. 482.
2. Fred Emery, *Watergate: The Corruption of American Politics and the Fall of Richard Nixon.* New York: Random House, 1994, p. xii.
3. Quoted in Carl Mollins, "A Modern Machiavelli," *Maclean's*, May 2, 1994, p. 30.

Chapter One: President Richard M. Nixon

4. Quoted in Anthony Summers, *The Arrogance of Power: The Secret World of Richard Nixon.* New York: Viking, 2000, p. 324.
5. Richard M. Nixon, *The Memoirs of Richard Nixon.* New York: Grosset and Dunlap, 1978, p. 12.
6. Quoted in Mel Elfin and Gary Cohen, "Richard M. Nixon," *U.S. News & World Report*, May 2, 1994, p. 24.
7. Quoted in "*Life* Remembers Richard M. Nixon," *Life*, June 19, 1994, p. 16.
8. Quoted in Summers, *The Arrogance of Power*, p. 16.
9. Quoted in Robert Dallek, *Nixon and Kissinger: Partners in Power.* New York: HaperCollins, 2007, p. 7.
10. Nixon, *The Memoirs of Richard Nixon*, p. 27.

11. Quoted in Summers, *The Arrogance of Power*, p. 45.
12. Quoted in Rick Perlstein, *Nixonland: The Rise of a President and the Fracturing of America.* New York: Scribner, 2008, p. 31.
13. Quoted in Dallek, *Nixon and Kissinger*, p. 19.
14. Quoted in Summers, *The Arrogance of Power*, p. 83.
15. Richard M. Nixon, Checkers speech, September 23, 1952, History Place Great Speeches Collection, www.historyplace.com/speeches/nixon-checkers.htm.
16. Quoted in Nixon, *The Memoirs of Richard Nixon*, p. 181.
17. Quoted in Summers, *The Arrogance of Power*, p. 218.
18. Quoted in Perlstein, *Nixonland*, p. 61.
19. Quoted in David Greenberg, *Nixon's Shadow: The History of an Image.* New York: Norton, 2003, p. 136.
20. Nixon, *The Memoirs of Richard Nixon*, p. 298.
21. Quoted in Tom Morganthau, "The Rise and Fall and Rise and Fall and Rise of Nixon." *Newsweek*, May 2, 1994, p. 24.

Chapter Two: The Break-In

22. Richard Nixon, first inaugural address, January 20, 1969, Yale Law

School, http://avalon.law.yale.edu/20th_century/nixon1.asp.

23. Quoted in Summers, *The Arrogance of Power*, p. 331.

24. Quoted in Summers, *The Arrogance of Power*, p. 332.

25. Quoted in Dallek, *Nixon and Kissinger*, p. 122.

26. Quoted in Emery, *Watergate*, p. 48.

27. Quoted in Richard Reeves, *President Nixon: Alone in the White House*. New York: Simon and Schuster, 2001, p. 353.

28. Nixon, *The Memoirs of Richard Nixon*, pp. 451–52.

29. Quoted in Reeves, *President Nixon*, p. 213.

30. Quoted in Perlstein, *Nixonland*, p. 387.

31. Quoted in *Time*, "The Plight of the Doves," *Time*, September 14, 1970, www.time.com/time/magazine/article/0,9171,902748,00.html.

32. Quoted in Theodore H. White, *Breach of Faith: The Fall of Richard Nixon*. New York: Atheneum, 1975, p. 158.

33. Quoted in Emery, *Watergate*, p. 118.

34. Quoted in G. Gordon Liddy, *Will*. New York: St. Martin's, 1980, p. 325.

35. Quoted in "Intruders in Democratic Headquarters," *Washington Post*, June 14, 1992.

36. Quoted in White, *Breach of Faith*, p. 160.

37. Quoted in Ben Bradlee Jr., "Watergate Celebrity No More," *Boston Globe*, April 30, 1983.

Chapter Three: The Cover-Up

38. Quoted in Stephen E. Ambrose, *Nixon Volume Two: The Triumph of a Politician 1962–1972*. New York: Simon and Schuster, 1989, p. 560.

39. Quoted in Reeves, *President Nixon*, p. 502.

40. Liddy, *Will*, p. 246.

41. Quoted in Emery, *Watergate*, p. 153.

42. Quoted in Carl Bernstein and Bob Woodward, *All the President's Men*. New York: Simon and Schuster, 1974, p. 18.

43. Alfred E. Lewis, "5 Held in Plot to Bug Democrats' Office Here," *Washington Post*, June 18, 1972.

44. Quoted in Perlstein, *Nixonland*, p. 678.

45. Quoted in Stanley I. Kutler, ed., *Abuse of Power: The New Nixon Tapes*. New York: Simon and Schuster, 1997, p. 67.

46. Quoted in Bernstein and Woodward, *All the President's Men*, p. 25.

47. Quoted in Perlstein, *Nixonland*, p. 678.

48. Quoted in Greenberg, *Nixon's Shadow*, p. 190.

49. Quoted in Kutler, *Abuse of Power*, p. 54.

50. Quoted in Greenberg, *Nixon's Shadow*, p. 190.

51. Nixon, *The Memoirs of Richard Nixon*, p. 717.

Chapter Four: A President Under Siege

52. Quoted in Summers, *The Arrogance of Power*, p. 324.

53. Quoted in Emery, *Watergate*, p. 239.

54. John J. Sirica, *To Set the Record Straight: The Break-in, the Tapes, the Conspirators, the Pardon*. New York: Norton, 1979, p. 88.

55. Quoted in Dallek, *Nixon and Kissinger*, 2007, p. 415.

56. Quoted in Reeves, *President Nixon*, p. 564.

57. Quoted in Gerald S. Strober and Deborah Hart Strober, *Nixon: An Oral History of His Presidency*. New York: HarperCollins, 1994, p. 430.
58. Quoted in Dallek, *Nixon and Kissinger*, p. 523.
59. Quoted in Bob Woodward, *Secret Man: The Story of Watergate's Deep Throat*. New York, Simon and Schuster, 2005, p. 93.
60. Quoted in Sirica, *To Set the Record Straight*, p. 96.
61. Quoted in Emery, *Watergate*, p. 269.
62. Quoted in Kutler, *Abuse of Power*, p. 247.
63. Quoted in Summers, *The Arrogance of Power*, p. 444.
64. Quoted in Liddy, *Will*, p. 278.
65. John Dean, *Blind Ambition: The White House Years*. New York: Simon and Schuster, 1976, p. 218.
66. Richard Nixon, Watergate speech, April 30, 1973, WWW Virtual Library, www.vlib.us/amdocs/texts/nixon041973.html.
67. Quoted in Emery, *Watergate*, p. 298.

Chapter Five: Hearings, Tapes, and Impeachment

68. Quoted in Kutler, *Abuse of Power*, p. 48.
69. Quoted in Reeves, *President Nixon*, p. 568.
70. Quoted in "A Few of the Sayings of Senator Sam," *San Francisco Chronicle*, April 24, 1985.
71. Quoted in George Lardner Jr., "Cox Is Chosen as Special Prosecutor, Democrat Served Under Kennedy as Solicitor General," *Washington Post*, May 19, 1973.
72. Quoted in Jules Witcover, "The First Day of Watergate: Not Exactly High Drama," *Washington Post*, May 18, 1973.
73. Quoted in White, *Breach of Faith*, p. 235.
74. Quoted in Elizabeth Drew, *Richard M. Nixon*. New York: Times Books, 2007, p. 114.
75. Quoted in Mike Feinsilber, "The Tapes That Ensnared—and Felled—a President," *Houston Chronicle*, www.chron.com/content/interactive/special/watergate/tapes.html.
76. Quoted in Sirica, *To Set the Record Straight*, pp. 137–38.
77. Quoted in Reeves, *President Nixon*, p. 605.
78. Quoted in Conrad Black, *Richard M. Nixon: A Life in Full*. New York: PublicAffairs, 2007, p. 937.
79. Quoted in Carroll Kilpatrick, "Nixon Tells Editors, 'I'm Not a Crook,'" *Washington Post*, November 18, 1973.
80. Quoted in Louis W. Liebovich, *Richard Nixon, Watergate, and the Press*. Westport, CT: Praeger, 2003, p. 102.
81. Nixon, *The Memoirs of Richard Nixon*, p. 993.
82. Barbara Charline Jordan, "Statement on the Articles of Impeachment," speech, delivered July 25, 1974, to the House Judiciary Committee, www.americanrhetoric.com/speeches/barbarajordanjudiciarystatement.htm.
83. Quoted in Alan Greenbalt, "The High Drama of Impeachment," *Congressional Quarterly Weekly Report*, August 12, 1995, p. 2,423.
84. Quoted in Nixon, *The Memoirs of Richard Nixon*, p. 1,073.
85. Quoted in Emery, *Watergate*, p. 470.
86. Nixon, *The Memoirs of Richard Nixon*, p. 1,078.

87. Richard Nixon, resignation speech, August 8, 1974, Public Broadcasting System, www.pbs.org/newshour/character/links/nixon_speech.html.

Chapter Six: The Aftermath

88. Quoted in Nixon, *The Memoirs of Richard Nixon*, p. 1,974.
89. Richard Nixon, final remarks at the White House, August 9, 1974, CNN, www.cnn.com/ALLPOLITICS/1997/gen/resources/watergate/nixon.farewell.html.
90. Gerald R. Ford, remarks on taking the oath of office as president, August 9, 1974, Gerald Ford Library and Museum, www.fordlibrarymuseum.gov/library/speeches/740001.html.
91. Ford, remarks on taking the oath of office as president.
92. Quoted in Leon Jaworski, *The Right and the Power: The Prosecution of Watergate*. New York: Reader's Digest Press, 1976, p. 227.
93. Quoted in Drew, *Richard M. Nixon*, p. 134.
94. Quoted in Berry Werth, "The Pardon," *Smithsonian*, February 2007, p. 56.
95. Gerald Ford, pardons Richard Nixon speech, September 8, 1974, CNN, www.cnn.com/ALLPOLITICS/1997/gen/resources/watergate/ford.speech.html.
96. Quoted in White, *Breach of Faith*, p. 343.
97. Quoted in Emery, *Watergate*, p. 180.
98. Sirica, *To Set the Record Straight*, p. 118.
99. Quoted in Stephen E. Ambrose, *Nixon: Ruin and Recovery 1973–1990*. New York: Simon and Schuster, 1992, p. 405.
100. Quoted in David Segal, "Interview with the Interviewer 'Frost/Nixon' Puts David Frost Back in the Public Eye," *Washington Post*, April 30, 2007.
101. Quoted in Drew, *Richard M. Nixon*, p. 138.
102. Quoted in Morganthau, "The Rise and Fall and Rise and Fall and Rise of Nixon," p. 24.
103. Henry Kissinger, remarks at the funeral services of President Nixon, April 27, 1994, Richard Nixon Library and Birthplace Foundation, www.nixonlibraryfoundation.org/index.php?src=gendocs&link=RNfuneral.
104. Quoted in Carroll Kilpatrick, "President Refuses to Turn Over Tapes; Ervin Committee, Cox Issue Subpoenas, Action Sets Stage for Court Battle on Powers Issue," *Washington Post*, July 24, 1973.
105. Quoted in Charles E. Claffey, "Sam Ervin; Nixon Still Owes Public a Confession," *Boston Globe*, June 17, 1982.
106. Quoted in Strober and Strober, *Nixon*, p. 505.
107. Quoted in Brooks Jackson, "A Watergate Legacy: More Public Skepticism, Ambivalence," CNN, June 12, 1997, www.cnn.com/ALLPOLITICS/1997/gen/resources/watergate/watergate.jackson.
108. Quoted in Strober and Strober, *Nixon*, p. 529.
109. Quoted in Kutler, *Abuse of Power*, p. 386.
110. Quoted in Reeves, *President Nixon*, p. 502.

For More Information

Books

Michael A. Genovese, *The Watergate Crisis*. Westport, CT: Greenwood Press, 1999. A thorough look at Watergate.

William S. McConnell, ed., *Watergate*. Farmington Hills, MI: Greenhaven Press, 2006. A collection of essays on various political issues involving Watergate.

Keith W. Olson, *Watergate: The Presidential Scandal That Shook America*. Lawrence: University Press of Kansas, 2003. A book that details every aspect of Watergate.

Peter C. Ripley, *Richard Nixon*. New York: Chelsea House, 1987. A biography of the nation's thirty-seventh president.

Web Sites

Gerald R. Ford Presidential Library & Museum (www.ford.utexas.edu). This Web site offers a number of online exhibits, including an extensive one on Watergate.

Watergate.info (www.watergate.info). This site offers articles, pictures, links to original documents, and analysis of the Watergate break-in and the political scandal that followed.

Index

Picture Credits

About the Author

Michael V. Uschan has written seventy books, including *Life of an American Soldier in Iraq*, for which he won the 2005 Council for Wisconsin Writers Juvenile Nonfiction Award. Uschan began his career as a writer and editor with United Press International, a wire service that provides stories to newspapers, radio, and television. Uschan considers writing history books a natural extension of the skills he developed in his many years as a journalist. He and his wife, Barbara, reside in the Milwaukee suburb of Franklin, Wisconsin.